# The School Psychology
# Licensure Exam Guide

**Peter D. Thompson, PhD, NCSP**, is a lead school neuropsychologist for Douglas County School District, which is a district of over 70 schools in Colorado. In addition to his responsibilities as a mentor and adviser to psychologists in Douglas County, Dr. Thompson is also the district's traumatic brain injury (TBI) team coordinator and regional liaison among the school district, government agencies, and organizations that serve families and students impacted by brain injuries. He lends his expertise in school neuropsychology to medical clinics and hospitals in the Denver metro area. Dr. Thompson holds several advanced psychology degrees with concentrations in educational psychology, school psychology, and school neuropsychology. He is the past president (2012) of the National Association of School Neuropsychology (NASN). Dr. Thompson authored the first edition of *The School Psychology Licensure Exam Guide* in 2004. He also helped write *Brain Injury in Children and Youth: A Manual for Educators* (2012) and *Concussion Guideline Manual* (2012) published by the Colorado Department of Education.

# The School Psychology Licensure Exam Guide
### Second Edition

*Peter D. Thompson, PhD, NCSP*

SPRINGER PUBLISHING COMPANY
NEW YORK

Springer Publishing Company, LLC
11 West 42nd Street
New York, NY 10036
www.springerpub.com

*Acquisitions Editor*: Nancy S. Hale
*Composition*: AMNET

*ISBN*: 978-0-8261-0989-7
*e-book ISBN*: 978-0-8261-0990-3

13 14 15 / 5 4 3 2 1

The author and the publisher of this Work have made every effort to use sources believed to be reliable to provide information that is accurate and compatible with the standards generally accepted at the time of publication. The author and publisher shall not be liable for any special, consequential, or exemplary damages resulting, in whole or in part, from the readers' use of, or reliance on, the information contained in this book. The publisher has no responsibility for the persistence or accuracy of URLs for external or third-party Internet websites referred to in this publication and does not guarantee that any content on such websites is, or will remain, accurate or appropriate.

**Library of Congress Cataloging-in-Publication Data**

Thompson, Peter D.
  The school psychology licensure exam guide / Peter D. Thompson, PhD. — Second edition.
    pages cm
  Includes bibliographical references and index.
  ISBN 978-0-8261-0989-7 (print edition : alk. paper) — ISBN 978-0-8261-0990-3 (e-book)
  1. School psychologists—Certification—United States—Examinations—Study guides.
  2. School psychology—United States—Examinations—Study guides.  3. School
psychology—United States—Examinations, questions, etc.  I. Title.
  LB3013.6.T56 2013
  371.7′13—dc23

                                                                    2012049729

Printed in the United States of America by Bradford & Bigelow.

# Contents

# Preface

*What lies behind us and what lies before
us are tiny matters compared to what
lies within us.*

*—Ralph W. Emerson*

After reading the epigraph, I assume that you, the reader, have something within you that drives you to help others. You have chosen to answer a difficult call to complete a highly demanding program of study and to seek your license as a school psychologist. Few people have accomplished this admirable feat, and you are about to join an elite, altruistic community of professional helpers. In my opinion, there is no higher calling than to serve others, especially children. Congratulations for answering the call and honoring the tiny matters that lie within you.

When preparing to tackle the licensure exam for school psychology, I diligently gathered as many resources as I could find. I queried several professors, utilized the Internet, and interviewed various graduate students. During this time, I was absolutely flabbergasted and dismayed at the paucity of information available to help me study.

Soon, my anxiety surrounding this vital test evolved into dread. After all, one could have stellar grades in graduate school but if you failed this one crucial exam, you would have no license to practice. In other words, this one test held the key to my occupational future. As it turned out, the exam's tough reputation and my thinking were faulty. The hype surrounding the test was just that: hype.

If you are a few months away from taking the licensure exam, then your primary enemy is probably anxiety. As future psychologists, we know that fear is born out of a lack of control or understanding of unknown events. Therefore, instead of letting your emotions detract from your abilities, harness the energy provided by this emotion to direct your actions to overcome the unknown. (And reread the above quote.) Additionally, you must moderate your worries by keeping in mind that the majority of people will pass the licensure exam, and you can always retake the test.

School psychology is built upon the simple tenet of helping others in need. Consequently, this guide endeavors to help future psychologists enter this worthy field. Although this guide is certainly not all-encompassing, I firmly believe that its information will assist aspiring school psychologists to prepare for the exam. However, it is important to understand that no single book or source holds all of the answers. The reader must utilize every resource possible, and this book is just one piece of the preparation pie.

Finally, there is a valuable concept I would like you to remember. The majority of test takers will soon be practitioners employed by large public school districts. Every year, millions of young students will also take important standardized tests that are just as stressful to them. If empathy is the hallmark of our profession, then let your test experience stew just a bit so you can truly understand how your future clients (i.e., students) feel when you evaluate them and ask them to take tests.

I wish the reader good luck, not only for passing the Praxis™ Exam but also in making a positive change in the lives of children.

# Acknowledgments

A person's achievements are most often attained with the guidance and support of others. The opportunity to research and write this second edition would have not been possible without the help of important people in my life. As a consequence, it is only right to acknowledge my family and colleagues who had a role in producing this book.

First, I would like to thank Dr. Colette Hohnbaum. Dr. Hohnbaum is not only a practicing school psychologist but is also an outstanding professor and leader in the Douglas County School District. Colette's insight and advice continue to be invaluable to me. Next, I must thank my wife, Michele, and daughter, Brooke, for their love and support. I cannot say too often how much they mean to me.

# Introduction

## Test Structure, General Suggestions, and Specific Advice

The primary benefit of this book is that it provides an excellent idea of the structure and content of *The Praxis Series™ School Psychologist Examination*, sometimes referred to as *The School Psychology Test* or *Praxis Exam*. This guide helps lift the veil of mystery surrounding how to pass this critical test necessary to become a licensed school psychologist. When people understand what to expect and have a solid strategy for approaching any task, not just a major test, their anxiety generally decreases. Additionally, when emotions are tamed, clarity of thought emerges and more cognitive energy can be devoted to higher-order reasoning, thus increasing the odds of success.

I have found the primary source of stress regarding the exam is the lack of good information related to test items and how to organize an effective study strategy. Trying to study for a comprehensive standardized psychology test is like studying for a history test. History is an incalculably broad subject with an equally endless amount of relevant information to study. The range of topics is so vast it seems overwhelming to even start preparing. However, the following chapters contain key suggestions and information that have helped thousands of other students pass the exam.

The suggestions in this book are based on interviews, remarks, and observations from professors, practicing school psychologists, and interns who have passed the exam. Some suggestions might be more useful than others. However, all advice and examples (even obvious ones) have been provided due to the various needs of different test takers. Also, it is extremely important to bear in mind that any statements made in this book are founded upon professional opinion and clinical practice. Although the advice in this guide is given out of sincerity to help the reader, the veracity of any comment or suggestion needs to be checked by the reader, if questioned. Remember, psychology is a dynamic and evolving field of study. Therefore, theories, best practices, and professional positions can change with time. Finally, it is important to note that the items and ideas contained in this book are not identical to the actual test questions or NASP (National Association of School Psychologists) study guides, but they are similar in content and format.

## How to Use This Guide

This guide was purposely written in a format that facilitates efficient studying, much like you would organize test notes in an outline structure. Previous test takers stated that information presented in a traditional book format, with long explanations, was too cumbersome. As a consequence of the concerns voiced by other students, I determined that the best means to present information to study for the Praxis Exam was through bulleted key concepts and lists.

To make effective use of your time, it is *not* necessary to memorize all theories and ideas in the realm of school psychology, which would be nearly impossible. Instead, the presented format is designed to help you know which concepts to memorize and which concepts need to be highly familiar. In general, you should memorize the ideas that are listed with numbers or letters. Also, any term or statement in boldface should be memorized. For other concepts that are bulleted, the reader does not necessarily need to commit them to long-term memory, but the ideas should become very familiar. With the previous comments in mind, always use your judgment when studying and know your areas of strength and areas where you need to allocate more effort. Finally, make good use of your time by reviewing the summary sections every night about 2 weeks before the exam.

## General Information and Test Format

To be employed as a licensed school psychologist in a public school, you must complete a school psychology degree program and pass the Praxis II National School Psychology Test (test code 0401). The licensure exam is administered by the Educational Testing Service (ETS), the same organization that provides public school teacher certifications and credentialing exams. Typically, a passing score of 165 is required for certification as a nationally certified school psychologist (NCSP), but a different score may be necessary for state licensure. Note that a school psychologist does not need to be an NCSP or a member of NASP to take this exam or practice psychology. However, the criteria for being an NCSP are typically higher than those without such a credential. Check with your state regulatory agency for more information on required test scores at www.ets.org/praxis/nasp. You can also check this website for official information on outlines, sample items with rationale for the best answers, and test-taking strategies.

The school psychology exam consists of 120 multiple-choice questions and lasts roughly 2 hours within a tightly controlled setting. Normally, each question has five response choices. (Answer choices are in A, B, C, D, E format.) Your chance of merely guessing correctly is 20%; not bad, but an educated guess significantly increases the odds of a correct answer. With the previous statistic in mind, the point is not to worry excessively about passing if you can provide an educated response on most items.

Although specific details about test construction and scoring are difficult to ascertain, it appears there are multiple versions or alternate forms of the Praxis Exam. Most likely, a large pool of questions and test items are used to construct different tests. In other words, the test changes with every administration. While you might have a few identical items on your test as a person from a previous group, it is unlikely you will get the same overall test used in a prior administration.

The content areas of the test are generally broken down into five domains. As the actual ETS test varies with each administration, it is likely that the number of questions associated with each domain also vary. On your exam, you might have more or fewer questions asked regarding each category. Also, keep in mind that all domains may share similar content and therefore specific test items could be placed in more than one domain. For example, a test question could ask about an intervention strategy that relies on general psychological principles; thus, that particular question has its roots in two domains (i.e., intervention and general psychological principles).

---

### Insider Tip

Graduate students who have taken the test stated that, despite what the ETS website asserts, the percentage of items from each domain seems different from test to test. For example, some test takers felt they had substantially fewer items from the *ethical and legal* domain but many more *assessment* domain questions than fellow classmates who took the exam a few weeks later. Because you do not know which domain might be emphasized on your exam, it is best to have a balanced approach when preparing for the exam and study each area equally. Of course it is always prudent to focus on areas that you know you are weak in.

---

## General Domains of the School Psychology Praxis Exam Format

The following information is an estimate of how the Praxis Exam was structured prior to 2008. Although this information is not definitive, the following estimates are based on interviews from students a few hours to a few days after taking the exam. Note the different terms used for the categories. Although the terms may have changed since 2008, the content is largely the same.

1. Assessments, Diagnosis, and Identification — 25% — (25–30 items)
2. Intervention and Prevention — 25% — (25–30 items)
3. General Psychological Principles — 20% — (20–25 items)
4. Education Principles and Methods — 10–15% — (10–15 items)
5. Laws and Ethics — 15–18% — (20–25 items)

This next section illustrates the current (post-2008) structure of the Praxis Exam, provided by ETS. The percentages are only estimates for the 120 multiple-choice items.

| | | |
|---|---|---|
| 1. Data-Based Decision Making | 35% | (42 items) |
| 2. Research-Based Behavioral and Mental Health Practices | 16% | (19 items) |
| 3. Applied Psychological Principles | 13% | (16 items) |
| 4. Research-Based Academic Practices | 12% | (14 items) |
| 5. Consultation and Collaboration | 12% | (14 items) |
| 6. Ethical, Legal, and Professional Foundations | 12% | (14 items) |

## Description of Categories

### I. Data-Based Decision Making (Assessment)

**A. Principles of Data-Based Decision Making**

Data Collection, Assessment Measures and Tests, Best Practices in Assessment, Working With Diverse and Special Populations

**B. Best Practices of Data-Based Decision Making**

Best Practices in Psychoeducational Services; Display of Data; Analysis of Progress Monitoring; Progress Monitoring in Reading, Writing, and Mathematics (Response to Intervention [RTI])

**C. Research and Program Evaluation**

Critiquing Tests, Employing Research in Practice, Evaluation Models and Methods

- **Example:** A large portion of questions that center on data-based decisions involve cognitive assessments, standardized measures, and informal data collection. These questions are typically straightforward and factual. For example, you might be asked, "Which subtest on the WISC-IV is not appropriate for visually impaired students?"

### II. Research-Based Behavioral and Mental Health Practices (Interventions)

**A. Primary, Secondary, and Tertiary Levels**

Preventative Strategies; Positive Behavior Support (PBS); Bully Prevention; Promoting Social, Emotional, and Academic Success; Classroom Organization and Management Growth; Service Learning

**B. School-Based Interventions, Skills, and Techniques**

Types of Individual and Group Counseling Techniques, Applied Behavioral Analysis, Psychoeducational Support

**C. Crisis Intervention, Prevention, and Response**

General Prevention Through Planning; Schoolwide Planning and Prevention; Specific Crisis Prevention, Intervention, and Response (bullying, suicide, death, and grief)

- **Example:** The questions nested under Research-Based Behavioral and Mental Health Practices are mostly related to counseling techniques, theories, and crisis intervention. Some questions are geared toward special education populations or specific strategies regarding individual intervention. An example question might be, "Which strategies are used to help a student with assertiveness issues?" (Answer: modeling, role playing, and rehearsal)

## III. Applied Psychological Principles

### A. Knowledge of General Principles

Theories of Intelligence, Theories of Development, Child Psychopathology, Substance Abuse, Pharmacology

### B. Knowledge of Measurement Theory

Types of Evaluations, Psychometrics (e.g., Reliability and Validity), Test Scores, Test Bias and Test Fairness, Assessment Procedures

- **Example:** The Applied Psychological Principles questions regard general principles related to psychometric testing and the field of psychology. A question within this domain might ask, "Which stage of Erik Erikson's psycho-social developmental theory addresses the middle childhood years (6 to 12 years old)?" (Answer: Stage Four: Industry versus Inferiority)

## IV. Research-Based Academic Practices

### A. Effective Instruction Practices

Instruction Strategies, Issues Related to Academic Successes and Problems, Education Policies and Practices, Retention, High-Stakes Testing

### B. Monitoring Interventions

Progress monitoring for reading, math, writing, and study skills

- **Example:** Research-based academic questions tend to focus on teaching practices and classroom-management techniques. This domain also covers how to properly monitor a student's progress. People who have little teaching experience might find this area challenging. An example question might be, "What is an effective method to teach and build comprehension skills?" (Answer: Have students ask themselves questions [self-talk] while reading a passage and predict the outcome.) It is important to remember that this particular domain may have similar questions to those in the general psychology or intervention domains.

## V. Consultation and Collaboration

### A. Models of Consultation and Collaboration

Know primary consultation models such as direct and indirect models. Also know key terms associated with consultation, such as *client* and *consultee*.

B. **Collaboration With Medical Personnel**

Medical experts and other agents who do not work specifically in schools can present special challenges. Understand how to communicate effectively with outside agencies and their special sets of issues.

C. **Working With Interpreters**

Effective consultation is predicated on effective rapport. Know the different ways to establish effective relationships. Once rapport is established, practitioners need to know the various models of consultation and when to employ specific consultation techniques with different specialists or personnel (e.g., medical staff and interpreters). Note that the major consultation models include behavioral, consultee-centered, instructional, and multicultural.

## VI. Ethical, Legal, and Professional Foundations

A. **Ethical Principles and Standards of Practice**

NASP Principles, NASP Professional Standards, Assessment Procedures, Laws and Regulations, Case Law (Court Cases)

B. **Professional Foundations of School Psychology**

Key Experts in the Field, Historical Milestones (Timeline)

- **Example:** Legal and ethical questions are sometimes given within a brief case-study or vignette format. Be familiar not only with specific case law (landmark rulings) but also the ramifications of the outcomes of such rulings. Many questions are also based on the Individuals with Disabilities Education Act (IDEA).

# Twenty-Five Tips for Studying and Preparing

1. Start studying early for the test. *Do not procrastinate.* Some people study a week before the test and soon realize that this was not enough time due to the vastness of the subject area. In my opinion, it is best to study for *at least* a month or more prior to the test. Your first few days will entail collecting and organizing information and notes. If you study 2 to 3 hours a day for a month, this will provide you with an adequate foundation.

2. Know when to study. There is some research that suggests studying before going to sleep is more effective than studying during the stress of the daytime. It might be best to study about an hour after eating dinner. Go for a walk after dinner to increase your oxygen intake and blood circulation to the brain. Studying from 7:00 p.m. to 10:00 p.m. then going to sleep is a good routine to follow.

3. Sleep is necessary for effective memory. Neuroscientists have valid research that links strong memory and retrieval of stored information to sound sleep. Lack of sleep causes a depletion of key neurochemicals in the limbic system that significantly hinders learning and memory. Make sure you are getting a solid 7 to 9 hours of sleep every night for several weeks before you take the test.

4. Hydration and diet play a vital role in brain health. Our brain is made mostly of fluid. You must make sure your brain is properly hydrated to maintain your performance. Students who are dehydrated have significant difficulties with focus, memory, and learning. Some researchers recommend a steady diet of water, bananas, and fish when studying. Do not overdo this diet but realize you might need to slightly increase your intake of healthy foods containing magnesium and omega-3 fatty acids.

5. Organize your notes and information according to the six broad categories listed previously. Have separate folders for each category. My own opinion is to have hard copies of your notes and outlines. Do not rely on your computer; you need backup documents. You might find it easier to have paper notes to quickly review information in the hours before the test.

6. Develop *keyword lists* and concise general-concept notes. I found this tip to be extremely helpful. Such lists make reviewing very time efficient and effective, especially a few days and hours before the actual test.

7. Study general concepts and keywords more than specific facts. *Familiarize* more than memorize. Although you certainly have to memorize several facts (e.g., specific case law, certain psychometric properties, psychological theories), understanding broad concepts provides a foundation that will enable you to answer most questions. For example, NASP's position on grade retention is that the practice is not a good idea in most cases. Your question on the test will usually be in the form of an example: "A parent comes to you and tells you her son has failed three classes in seventh grade and wants to retain him. What is your response?" In such a case, your response should be to determine if something is interfering with the child's learning (e.g., social or emotional problems, learning difficulties) and to suggest various options that will allow the child to make up the subjects, such as summer school. Notice how the previous question does not explicitly ask about NASP's position on grade retention.

8. If you choose to study with a group, keep the group small. Study groups are effective if they are *kept small* (three to four people). With too many people, focusing the group and socializing become issues. *Do not overemphasize study groups*. Meet just a few times with the group to exchange information and quiz each other. Everyone within the small group should bring completed outlines and notes to the first meeting. Group members should have copies of their outlines to share. Although this is more work than dividing tasks up among individual members, information gathered this way is more comprehensive and usually stimulates meaningful conversations about relevant test items.

   *Note:* Trust yourself to study alone. You may not need a study group but rather just a few consultation sessions with a few colleagues or your professor. Sometimes groups can be too demanding, so be guarded with your time and use it effectively.

9. Secure an undergraduate "Introduction to Psychology" textbook and read the summaries for each chapter. The textbook should be no more than 5 years old. Such textbooks are excellent for reviewing the newest general psychological theories and research. Most introductory psychology texts also have excellent

chapters on psychopathology, neuropsychology, and psychometrics. Additionally, these books are easy to digest, and key concepts are presented in a thorough manner.

10. It may be appropriate to study your weak content areas, but be careful how you emphasize any one area. Some students may spend most of their time studying specific case laws. However, these students studied one area at the expense of other information that is just as important. For example, some students may have only two case law questions but have four psychometric questions. If you feel you are weak in one of the six domain areas, by all means spend a little more time on that material to bolster your weakness. However, do not skimp on studying an area because you think it is your strength.

11. Read chapter summaries from major textbooks you purchased during your program of study. Again, be very familiar with broad concepts and memorize only key facts. Be very judicious in what you decide to memorize. Do not spend too much time reading entire chapters unless you are very weak in that area. Recommended textbooks include Jerome Sattler's books on cognitive and behavioral assessments and Randy Kamphaus's works on similar information.

12. Read chapter summaries and abstracts from NASP's *Best Practices in School Psychology*. Many graduate students attempt to read the entire *Best Practices* book. While this is useful, it is highly time-consuming, and large sections of this book will not be on the test. After speaking with colleagues who took the exam, they told me that reading the summaries and a few specific chapters was most effective. I found reading chapters that dealt with multicultural issues, testing, interventions (counseling), and consultation to be helpful.

13. Be familiar with key acronyms. You do not necessarily have to memorize them, but be able to recognize an acronym and be familiar with its importance.

14. Take as many practice tests as possible and discuss missed items with your study group. If you have an effective study group, have each member create a mini-test. Swap tests and discuss them at your next session. Taking practice tests is the best way to initially reduce test anxiety. It will also prepare your mind for taking timed tests. Prepare by taking the two practice tests located at the back of this guide.

15. When taking the exam, practice effective time management. To my knowledge, all questions are scored equally. Therefore, do not spend too much time on any one particular item. There are 120 questions to answer in 2 hours. I am a slow test taker and had 15 minutes to spare at the end.

16. If you decide not to take the electronic version of the exam and take the paper version instead, bring several extra pencils with high-quality erasers to the test.

17. Never leave any question unanswered. Usually, you will be able to quickly narrow down your test answer to two choices. If you have difficulty choosing an answer, put a small mark by the question and give it a good guess. If time permits at the end, go back and examine the marked question again. (There is some debate about whether a person's first guess is the most accurate.)

18. Allow yourself time at the end of the test to recheck your answers. If you have been taking practice tests, you should have honed your time-management skills. If you have extra time when you complete your test, you should do two things. First, review the entire test and make sure each oval within the multiple-choice format is cleanly filled. Stray marks or messy corrections might interfere with scoring—this is very important. Second, reread the questions you had difficulty answering and see if other test items might provide help. During my test, I noticed that one test item contained information that helped answer another item that I had trouble answering.

19. Go to the NASP website and read about NASP's position papers and best practices. NASP endorses certain practices and provides guidelines for practitioners. For example, NASP has strong opinions regarding the use of punishment to correct student behaviors.

20. If you are going to take a blind guess answering a question, some of my colleagues suggest that it is best to guess "C" or "D." However, if I can match a keyword in the choice section to anything in the question, I usually answer accordingly.

21. Register to take the test as early as possible. You will be able to register early through the Internet. If you do not register early, you run the risk of not being able to take the test in a convenient location. Some people might have to drive a very long distance to take the test. Remember to double-check your university's code, which you will have to enter. If you put in the wrong code, your school will not receive your scores. A few weeks after the test, a copy of your scores will be sent to your home, and a breakdown of how you performed on each section of the test will be detailed.

22. Allow yourself to miss a few questions without stressing about it. Remember, you can miss several items and still pass the test. Do not be a perfectionist or think you have to know it all. For practical purposes, there is no difference between getting 70% correct and 100% correct; both scores pass and nobody asks you your scores after you graduate.

23. When studying general psychological theories and concepts, focus on those parts that are relevant only to the age group of 5- to 18-year-olds. For example, be more familiar with Erikson's psychosocial stages for children rather than for the adults.

24. On the test day, relax, relax, and relax. Your emotions and anxiety will be elevated on the day you take the test. Some anxiety is helpful, but not too much. If you have sincerely prepared for the test, then do not second guess your efforts; you are prepared. Follow your normal routine the day of the test. Always remember that you can *retake* the test if you do not perform as well as you expected. In fact, some people study for the NASP test by taking it twice. When I took the test, I told myself beforehand that I would arrive about half an hour early and only review keywords and concepts. After reviewing once, that was it. I simply enjoyed my coffee and waited for the test to begin.

25. Finally, eat a decent dinner and get a full night's sleep before the test. The day before the exam, review your notes but do not stress or try to learn new

material. As mentioned, it is important to hydrate yourself by drinking an extra glass of water. The brain needs water to think effectively.

## Insider Observations

The following notes from students who took the exam are provided to give you a general idea of how some tests are structured. You may find that your test is not exactly the same as the following comments indicate. However, you may have several similar items and questions.

- One test had 15 long scenario-type questions. Scenario questions are comprised of 7- to 12-sentence paragraphs. After reading the short paragraph, you have to choose the best answer from four to five choices.

- Of the 15 scenario questions, three or four of the scenarios had multiple questions ammended to them. For example, one vignette accounted for questions numbered 65 through 68.

- Several questions on the exam were about one to three short sentences in length. These questions asked for straightforward information. For example, "Carl Rogers is best known for what?"

- For approximately 75% of the questions I was able to very quickly narrow down the choices to two responses. The two narrowed-down responses seemed to have kernels of truth in both of them. Take the best educated guess and look for keywords that match your answer to the question.

- Roughly 65% of the questions were short-example types that ask you to apply your knowledge. For example, "You have a new student who was referred for anxiety problems around test taking. What should you do first?" (Answer: Secure signed permission from the parents to counsel the student.)

- The majority of test takers completed the test with about 20 minutes to spare. It is estimated that about 66% of your colleagues will finish with about 20 minutes to spare.

- It seemed two or three questions on the exam helped to answer a few other items because of the information they contained. Sometimes keywords in the choices will remind you of concepts and other important ideas.

- Very few, if any, items have tricky or multiple answers. For example, I did not have a choice that read, "A and C are true but B is not."

# 1

# First Test Section: Data-Based Decision Making

By no means does this guide contain everything you need to know about school psychology. As school psychologists, we are busy practitioners who must keep abreast of several new developments within the various subfields of psychology, not just our own area. We must know concepts in psychometrics, neuropsychology, counseling psychology, social psychology, educational psychology, and other branches of our discipline.

Despite the vastness of the psychological arena, this chapter, as well as subsequent chapters, provides some of the psychometric principles and specific facts you need for a starting point and foundation to prepare for your exam. Again, I must emphasize that using multiple streams of information is the best approach in your studies, especially in the area of data-based decision making. The majority of test items related to data-based decision making asks you to *apply* your knowledge, rather than to repeat back psychological trivia.

## Data-Based Decision Making

**What Is Data-Based Decision Making?** Data-based decision making involves the collection of formal and informal information. Initially, information gathered on a struggling student is linked to the school's response to intervention (RTI) process. If the student continues to struggle despite the best efforts of the RTI team, a full and comprehensive evaluation is conducted. Before the revised edition of the Praxis™ Exam, data-based decision-making questions centered largely on standardized testing and assessments. You will still have several test questions regarding formal cognitive tests and behavioral assessments, but RTI questions have significantly increased over the past few years.

Informal and formal data are required to inform professional judgments regarding an individual student at the following levels:

1. **Background Data Collection and Problem Identification Level:** You must know various methods of data collection to help identify and *define* the problem.

2. **Screening Level:** Data can be used to help identify at-risk students and make decisions about students who struggle with academic work.

3. **Progress Monitoring and RTI Level:** Data is used to determine effectiveness of the interventions (RTI) once a student is identified.

4. **Formal Assessment Level (Special Education Evaluation):** Cognitive, social, and emotional data is derived from various sources, but especially from formal standardized measures.

In general, data is used for the following needs:

1. To identify the problem and plan interventions
2. To increase or decrease levels of intervention
3. To help determine whether interventions are implemented with fidelity
4. To decide whether interventions are related to positive student outcomes (effectiveness)
5. To plan individualized instruction and strategic long-term educational planning

## I. Background Data Collection, Techniques, and Problem Identification

When a struggling student has been identified already through various means, the initial data collected should help define the problem. Remember to collect data with an emphasis on the referral question (e.g., What is the area in which the student is having difficulty?). Initial data collection sources include background information, interviews, and observations.

A. **Collection and Analysis of Vital Background Information (Informal Data)**

1. Student files and records
2. Staff interviews and comments about the student
3. Medical records and reports
4. Review of previous interventions
5. Developmental history

B. **Interview and Interview Techniques**

**Student interviewing:** It is important to reference the following resource of information on child interviewing: www.nasponline.org/publications/spr/pdf/spr182hughes.pdf

1. **Structured interviews** are more standardized and formal. The same questions are given to each child.

 • **Advantages**: Structured interviews have high validity and reliability. Children's responses can be directly compared to other children's responses. Structured diagnostic interviews indicate the presense or absense of a problem, not level of functioning.

 • **Limitations**: Generally, the interviewer is unable to modify questions to the needs of the interviewee. The interview must follow a strict format and administration.

2. **Unstructured interviews** are based on the assumption that converational style helps to put the student at ease. The less you put structure on the child the more the child will share.

   - **Advantage**: Unstructured interviews can be adapted to the needs of the interviewee.
   - **Limitations**: Child responses can be difficult to interpret. The responses cannot be compared to norms as seen within the more structured interview measures.

3. **Semi-structured interviews** combine the best features of both structured and unstructured interviews. They allow for flexibility and follow-up questions.

C. **Observational Techniques**

Observational techniques are used to observe and record behavior in a natural setting.

1. **Whole-interval recording**: Behavior is only recorded when it occurs during the entire *time interval*. (This is good for continuous behaviors or behaviors occurring in short duration.)

2. **Frequency or event recording**: Record the *number* of behaviors that occurred during a specific period.

3. **Duration recording** refers to the *length of time* the specific behavior lasts.

4. **Latency recording:** Time between onset of stimulus or signal that initiates a specific behavior.

5. **Time sampling interval recording**: Select a time period for observation, divide period into a number of equal intervals, and record whether or not behavior occurs. Time sampling is effective when the beginning and end of behavior are difficult to determine or when only a brief period of time is available for observation.

6. **Partial-interval recording**: Behavior is scored if it occurs during any part of the time interval. Multiple episodes of behavior in a single time interval are counted as one score or mark. Partial-interval recording is effective when behaviors occur at a relatively low rate or for inconsistent durations.

7. **Momentary time sampling**: Behavior is scored as present or absent only during the moment that a timed interval begins. This is the least biased estimate of behavior as it actually occurs.

## II. Screening Measures and Methods

**Universal Screening:** Universal screening is broadly implemented and it is systematic. Universal assessment of *all* children can be done within a given class, grade, school, or district on academic, behavioral, social, or emotional indicators that the school and community have agreed are critical for success.

1. **Purpose:** The **broad** purpose of universal screening is to help determine whether modifications are needed in the core curriculum, instruction, or general education environment. Second, the **narrow** purpose is to guide decisions about additional or intensive instruction for those specific students who may require instructional support beyond what is already provided at a broad level.

2. **Benefits and Liabilities of Screeners:** Universal screening tools are cost effective, time efficient, and easy to administer. However, there is a chance of misclassifying some students when using screening tools. It is better to err on the side of false positives so as to provide additional support to a student who may not need it rather than to deny additional support to a student in need as a result of a false negative. This is referred to as the **least dangerous assumption**.

**Universal Screening Measures:**

1. **Curriculum-based measures (CBM)** are typically reliable but must only be used if they align with local norms, benchmarks, and standards. An example of CBM would be a reading fluency measure such as DIBELS (Dynamic Indicators of Basic Early Literacy Skills).

2. Fluency-based indicators of skills are common universal screeners. Such screeners include initial-sound fluency, letter-naming fluency, phoneme segmentation, nonsense-word fluency, and oral-reading fluency.

3. The **Cognitive Assessment Test (CogAT)** is a cognitive measure, but it is group administered and qualifies as a screener.

4. State educational agencies employ formal group-administered tests that are given to students every year to monitor student growth in reading, writing, and math. Some school districts use alternatives to a state-created test, such as the Iowa Test of Basic Skills.

5. Schools using the **System to Enhance Educational Performance (STEEP)** conduct CBMs in reading, math, and writing several times a year to identify students in need of additional support.

## III. Progress Monitoring and Response to Intervention (RTI) Level

Several effective data-tracking programs and procedures have been created to record and analyze a student's historical test results in specific academic areas, such as reading, math, and spelling. The reader should be familiar with well-known RTI tracking programs such as AimsWeb.

In general, the RTI process is as follows. Typically, a student is identified with an academic or behavioral concern (or both) by his or her teacher or parent. After a student has been identified, the school psychologist utilizes the first two steps of the information-gathering process (i.e., data collection and screening information). Once a student's problem area is clearly defined, baseline data is collected on the student's specific area of concern. Next, research-based interventions are employed and systematic tests are provided to measure the student's postintervention progress. The student's test data are formally documented, tracked, and analyzed. After several points of intervention data are collected, an analysis is conducted that examines the difference between the student's initial baseline performance and the expected level of performance after interventions have been implemented. It is expected that the majority of students should respond to the new intervention in age-expected ways, meaning the student should make progress and close the gap between baseline data and age-expected data. However, if the student does not grow due to faithful implementation of the intevention in a reasonable amount of time (30 to 60 days), then a special education evaluation should be considered.

A. **Best practices in deciding *what* to assess**:

There are two levels of collecting progress-monitoring data:

1. **Subskill Mastery Measurement (SMM)**—Information on student progress is collected to determine whether the *specific* intervention for the target behavior is effective. SMM data should be collected frequently, even daily.

2. **General Outcome Measurement (GOM)**—Data are collected to determine whether the student is making progress toward long-range goals. GOMs are used less frequently than SMM, such as once a week.

B. **Best practices in deciding *how* to assess and present data:**

1. Progress-monitoring data should be based on the *systematic and repeated* measurement of behavior over a specified time.

2. Frequency data, percentage correct, or number of opportunities to respond are the results that are typically recorded and displayed.

3. The horizontal axis on a graph typically represents real and appropriate intervals of time (e.g., days or weeks).

4. *Note:* There will be **three levels of analysis**.

   a. Analysis of the **variability** in data

   b. Analysis of **level**

   c. Analysis of **trend**

C. **Best practices in *analyzing* variability of progress-monitoring data:**

• **Variability and sources of error**: Each progress-monitoring data point has important considerations and sources of variability.

1. The first cause of data variability centers on the effectiveness of the intervention. Whether an intervention is effective or not is defined by its ability to change behavior. A change in behavior should be observed and measured in the progress-monitoring data.

2. A second source of variability is called a *confounding* variable, which includes uncontrolled subject and environmental variables. Controlling these extraneous variables whenever possible is necessary to ensure that the effectiveness of the intervention is what is actually measured.

3. The third source of variability is measurement error. Measurement error can occur if, for example, an observer was not looking when the target behavior occurred or if a CBM probe was not administered properly.

• **Consideration of mitigating factors:** If extraneous variables are not considered, then student performance may be attributed to the intervention when the changes might be due to the effects of uncontrolled personal or environmental variables.

- **RTI analysis of *level*:**

  *Level* refers to the average performance within a condition.

  Example: A condition occurs when a student's performance changes suddenly following a change in conditions. A student's level of performance is often compared to the average level of performance of peers or to a benchmark level.

- **RTI analysis of *trend*:**

  1. When a student's performance systematically increases or decreases across time, then analyzing the trend in the data is important. The pattern of change in a student's behavior *across time* can be described as *trend*.

  2. Multiple measurements are required to estimate a trend. Statistical methods can be used to calculate the slope or trend line. Slope is easily calculated with most statistical and spreadsheet software (e.g., SPSS) and the resulting trend line can be plotted on a graph.

  3. Visual analysis can also be used to estimate the general pattern of change across time. **Caution**: It is important to determine whether the overall pattern in the data is consistent and linear across time or whether another pattern (e.g., nonlinear, curvilinear) better explains the data.

- **Describing and analyzing baseline RTI data:**

  Progress-monitoring data are first collected during *baseline* to determine the current level, trend, and variability of behavior. Baseline is the condition *prior* to intervention.

  - **General RTI Evaluation Points:**

    1. One rule for baseline data is that there should be no new highs (spikes) or lows for *three* consecutive data points.

    2. Another rule is that **80% of the data points should fall within 15% of the mean (average)** line or, in the case of increasing or decreasing data points, within 15% of the trend line.

    3. Some researchers recommend collecting a minimum number of baseline data points, approximately three to five points.

    4. In schools, practical considerations often affect the amount of data that can be collected.

D. **Best practices for making decisions based on RTI data:**

   The three characteristics used to describe behavior (level, trend, and variability) may change because of the introduction of an intervention. Initially, it is important to consider if a sufficient number of data points exists in each condition to obtain an accurate picture of the behavior under both the baseline and intervention conditions. Next, determine if the change in behavior closely coincides with the change in conditions. An immediate change in the level, trend, or variability of the behavior is likely the result of the intervention.

- **RTI decision rules**

  **Reasons to Use RTI Data:** Students whose teachers use data-based decisions learn more than students whose teachers do not rely on such data. To make data-based decisions you must first have a goal that is based on local norms, benchmarks, or classroom-comparison norms. The following are decision rules to use with RTI data.

1. **Should the intervention be changed?**

   If two or three data points during the intervention condition fall below the *aim* line, the intervention needs to be changed. You should analyze the trend line over the last several data points and compare it to the aim line. If the slope of the student's trend line is less than the slope of the aim line, the intervention needs to be changed.

2. **Are there no correct responses for 3 or more days (or sessions) in a row?**

   If there are no correct responses for three to four sessions, change the intervention.

3. **Are the data highly variable?**

   Consider extraneous factors when data is too variable. Examples of extraneous factors include the difficulty of the probes, different examiners, failing to get a student's attention before presenting stimuli, student noncompliance, insufficient reinforcement for correct responding, or level of motivation.

4. **Is the percentage of correct responding below 85%?**

   To correct this problem include modifications to the instruction by providing better prompts, additional modeling, or more effective corrective feedback.

5. **Is the student's performance accurate but slow?**

   If growth is slow, focus efforts on increasing the student's rate of correct responses. Rate increase is achieved through repeated practice and systematic contingencies to address student motivation.

## IV. Formal Evaluation Level (Special Education Evaluation)

If a student fails to show a proper response to interventions, a more comprehensive evaluation is need to help better understand the nature of the student's difficulty and to plan for more intensive support services. At this last level, scientific and standardized tests are typically employed. It is important to know that school psychologists are required to *use both qualitative and quantitative data* in their analaysis for determination of special education eligiblity. Although qualitative data are vital, the complex nature of formal psychological tests, procedures, and statistics makes the quantitative aspect more challenging. The reader should be well versed in psychometrics and ready to answer hypothetical case questions regarding test statistics and specific problems associated with formalized test data. For example, on the Praxis Exam, you may be asked, "Which specific test would be best to administer or why is a particular test not a valid choice to use?" Another question might ask, "Why should a school psychologist not use the Differential Abilities Scale (DAS)-I?" Answer: Because standardized tests with *norms older than 10 years* should be used with caution.

- Although the following Internet resource is designed to assist psychologists when evaluating students with brain injuries, the assessment area of this webpage provides you with a comprehensive list and description of specific formal subtests that can be used to evaluate a variety of cognitive functions such as memory, learning, attention, and reasoning. Make sure to double click on the area you are interested in assessing with a formal test. Go to the following link: http://cokidswithbraininjury.com/educators-and-professionals/information-matrix

- A comprehensive special education evaluation will include formal and informal data within each of the following major domains:
  - Cognitive ability
  - Achievement
  - Communication (speech/language)
  - Motor skills
  - Adaptive skills
  - Social, emotional, and behavioral functioning
  - Sensory processing
- Be familiar with the following common assessment instruments and tests. The following tests are typically ones that are administered by school psychologists. Generally speaking, the first four or five are most common in each category and most likely seen on the Praxis Exam.

A. **Common Measures of Cognitive Function (in order of popular use)**
  - WISC-IV (6 to16 years and 11 months)
  - Differential Abilities Scales-II (2.5 years to 17 years 11 months)
  - Stanford-Binet IV (2 to 85+ years)
  - WPPSI-IV (2.5 to 7.5 years)
  - WAIS-V (16 to 74 years)
  - Woodcock-Johnson Test of Cognitive Ability (2 to 90 years)
  - Bayley Scales of Infant Development (1 to 42 months)
  - Leiter (2 to 20 years)
  - Kaufman Assessment Battery for Children, Second Edition (KABC-II) (3 to 18 years)
  - Kaufman Adolescent and Adult Intelligence test (11 to 85+ years)
  - Universal Nonverbal Intelligence Test (UNIT) (5 to 17 years and 11 months)

B. **Common Measures of Educational Achievement**
  - Woodcock-Johnson Test of Achievement-III (2 to 90 years)
  - Wide Range Achievement Test (WRAT-4) (5 to 94 years)
  - Kaufman Test of Educational Achievement (K-TEA) (grades 1 to 12)
  - Wechsler Individual Achievement Test (WAIT) (4 to 50 years 11 months)

The following are early childhood achievement tests:
  - Test of Early Reading Ability (TERA)
  - Test of Early Math Ability (TEMA)
  - Kaufman Survey of Early Academic and Language Skills (K-SEALS)

C. **Neuropsychological Measures (Basic Neuropsychological Functions)**
*Note:* Several basal neurological processes can be assessed by using a cross-battery approach. For example, to measure processing speed, subtests from the DAS-II can be employed. Common basal neurological processes include, memory, attention, processing speed, and sensory. Higher order reasoning is generally assessed by cognitive test batteries, not neuropsychological tests.

- **Memory Tests**
  - Wechsler Memory Scale
  - Test of Memory and Learning (TOMAL-2)
  - Working Memory scales of WISC-IV, DAS-II, WCJ-Cog, SB-IV
  - Wide Range Assessment of Memory and Learning, Second Edition (WRAML2)
- **Executive Functioning and Attention (after age 8)**
  - BRIEF (Standardized survey of questions)
  - CAS-Attention and Planning domains
  - Delis-Kaplan Executive Function System (D-KEFS)
  - NEPSY (Attention—Executive Functions Domain)
  - Behavioral Assessment of Dysexecutive Syndrome (BADS)
  - Wisconsin Card Sort Test (WCST)
  - Rey Complex Figure Test (RCFT) (also taps visual–perceptual and memory)
  - Conner's Continuous Performance Test
  - Tower Tests (e.g., Tower of London)
- **Phonemic Awareness Tests**
  - Comprehensive Test of Phonological Processing (CTOPP)
  - Test of Phonological Awareness—Kindergarten
  - Nonword Spelling (Screening)
  - Yopp–Singer Test of Phoneme Segmentation
  - Rosner Auditory Analysis Test
  - Rapid Name and Phoneme Segmentation, such as Dynamic Indicators of Basic Early Literacy Skills (DIBELS)
  - DAS-II Phonological Processing domain
- **Language Tests**
  - Peabody Picture Vocabulary Test (2 to 90+ years)
  - Various verbal reasoning subtests from major cognitive test batteries, such as the WISC-IV or DAS-II
- **Visual Processes**
  - Beery–Buktenica Developmental Test of Visual–Motor Integration
  - DAS-II Recall of Designs
  - Rey Complex Figure Test (RCFT)

- **Major Neuropsychological Test Batteries (Comprehensive)**
  - NEPSY-II
  - D-KEFS

## D. Emotional, Behavioral, and Social Skills Measures

- **Informal Measures for Social and Emotional Problems:** Multiple data sources should be used, such as the number of office referrals, suspensions, and classroom-based disciplinary procedures. These can be used to detect preexisting levels of problem behaviors. These outcomes represent indirect measures of social skills as these outcomes are presumed to reflect corresponding levels of prosocial behavior.
  - **Internet resources for more social and emotional information:**

    Collaborative for Academic, Social, and Emotional Learning: http://www.casel.org

    Center for the Social Emotional Foundations of Early Learning: http://csefel.vanderbilt.edu

- **Functional Behavioral Assessment (FBA):** A functional behavioral assessment is a comprehensive and individualized strategy to identify the purpose or function of a student's problem behavior(s). FBAs are used to develop a plan to modify factors that maintain the problem behavior and teach appropriate replacement behaviors using positive interventions.
  - **Key aspects of an FBA:** Antecedents (A), Behavior (B), and Consequences (C)
  - **Steps to complete an FBA:**
    1. Describe problem behavior (operationally define problem).
    2. Perform the assessment. (Review records; complete systematic observations; and interview student, teacher, parents, and other needed individuals.)
    3. Evaluate assessment results. (Examine patterns of behavior and determine the purpose or function of the target behaviors.)
    4. Develop a hypothesis.
    5. Formulate an intervention plan.
    6. Start or implement the intervention.
    7. Evaluate effectiveness of intervention plan.

    *Note:* Current research and practice informs psychologists to place emphasis on the *antecedents* of a behavior. Determine what is triggering the behavior in the environment. What can you change in the environment to make the target behavior less likely to occur?
  - **Internet resources for more FBA information:**

    www.usu.edu/teachall/text/behavior/LRBIpdfs/Functional.pdf

    http://cecp.air.org/fba/problembehavior2/main2.htm

- **Common standardized measures to evaluate social and emotional development or problematic areas:**

  **Note:** Effective social and emotional measures include at least two forms, typically a parent form and teacher form. Best practice is to have multiple raters and results should be largely congruent.

  - BASC-2 (Three Forms: Self, Teacher, Parent)
  - Devereux Scales of Mental Disorders (Forms: Teacher, Parent)
  - Revised Behavior Problem Checklist (RBPC) (Forms: Parent, Teacher)
  - Reynolds Adjustment Screening Inventory—Adolescent
  - Conner's Rating Scales-Revised
  - Beck Depression Inventory-II
  - Revised Children's Manifest Anxiety Scales, Second Edition

E. **Additional Measurement and Assessment Considerations**

- **Curriculum-Based Assessment (CBA):** CBA is a term used to describe a broad assessment program or process, which may include CBMs or structured observations.

- **Curriculum-Based Measurement (CBM):** CBM refers to the specific forms of criterion-referenced assessments in which curriculum goals and objectives serve as the "criteria" for assessment items.

  - **Top Characteristics of Effective CBM**

    1. CBMs must be based on *systematic* procedures for the *frequent* collection and analysis of student performance data.

    2. The key to CBM is the examination of student performance *across time* to evaluate intervention effectiveness.

    3. CBM is a system to identify students who are *at risk.*

    4. CBM provides *normative and statistically sound information* for students, classes, staff, and parents.

  - **Examples of CBM in Content Areas:**

    1. Reading: Students read aloud for 2 minutes from a passage of text. The number of words read correctly and incorrectly are counted and compared to the class average.

    2. Spelling: Students complete a 2-minute spelling test with words presented at 10-second intervals. Words are randomly selected from the students' spelling curriculum. The number of correct words or letter sequences are counted and compared to the class average.

    3. Math: Students complete a 3-minute grade-level computational exercise. Correct answers are counted and analyzed against other peers in class.

    4. Writing: Students are asked to listen to a short passage and write for 2 minutes about the contents of the passage. The number of correct or on-topic sentences is counted and compared.

F. **Authentic (Ecological) Assessments**

- Ecological assessments are just as important as formal or standardized assessments. Ecological assessments help to determine the "goodness of fit" between the student and the learning environment.

- An important acronym to remember is **ICEL**. ICEL stands for instruction, curriculum, environment, and learner. During an ecological assessment, the evaluator must review key elements of the four aspects of ICEL. For example, a school psychologist analyzes work samples, prior grades, and assessments. Information from parents, teachers, and the student is collected. Finally, authentic assessments include observational data of the target student during instruction and in other environments.

G. **Assessing Intellectual Disabilities (ID or Mental Retardation)**

- Assessment of children with an intellectual disability, which was known previously as mental retardation, requires *both* cognitive and adaptive measures.

- Significantly below average *intellectual* functioning is a critical criterion. A **standard score of 70** or below on an individually administered cognitive test such as the WISC-IV or other similar test is needed for a diagnosis.

- Origins of the disability must be prior to age 18.

- Child must demonstrate deficits or impairments in present *adaptive* functioning (i.e., the person's effectiveness in meeting the standards expected for his or her age by his or her cultural group) in at least **two** of the following areas:

  a. Communication

  b. Self-care and home living

  c. Social skills

  d. Use of community resources

  e. Self-direction (ability to be independent)

  f. Functional academic skills

  g. Employment

  h. Leisure

  i. Physical health issues

  **Note:** Common adaptive-functional measures used by school psychologists are the Vineland and ABAS.

H. **Assessment of Non-English-Speaking or Special Populations (English Language Learners (ELL) or English as a Second Language (ESL)**

  1. When evaluating language competency, you must assess speaking, reading, and writing abilities while considering the child's:

     a. Developmental history and all languages that are spoken and heard

     b. Language dominance (the language the student has heard the most in his or her environment)

     c. Language preference

2. Language proficiency in *both* languages must be assessed and the dominant language must be determined. Such information is crucial to the interpretation of any assessment data that is gathered.

3. Guidelines for distinguishing language *differences* from language *disorders*:

   a. The disorder must be present in the child's native language (L1) and English (L2).

   b. Testing must be conducted in the native or strongest language.

   c. Assessments must be conducted using both formal and informal measures. When possible, it is important to use formal measures that have been normed on the appropriate cultural group (e.g., Spanish WISC).

   d. Language must be assessed in a variety of formal and informal speaking contexts.

   e. Patterns of language usage must be described and error patterns must be determined.

   f. The child's language performance must be compared to that of other bilingual speakers who have had similar cultural and linguistic experiences. The child should be compared to members of the same cultural group who speak the dialect.

   ***Note:*** Make sure to review possible factors that contribute to the interruption of language development. Such factors may include socioeconomic status (SES), poor instruction, lack of experience or exposure to language, school attendance, and so on.

4. Considerations When Using Standardized Tests for Second-Language Learners

   ***Note:*** The *first bullet is most important*, and you only need to be familiar with the rest of the points; it is not necessary to memorize them.

   • Remember that the use of standardized tests with direct test translation (use of an interpreter) is not best practice and is psychometrically very weak if the test is not normed on the cultural group being assessed.

   • When using standardized tests, recognize that norming samples are not stratified on the basis of bilingual ability and are rarely applicable to the majority of students being assessed, thus invalidating scores.

   • The use of an interpreter can assist in collecting information and administering tests, however, score validity *remains low* even when the interpreter is highly trained and experienced.

   • Use systematic methods based on established research for collecting and interpreting data in a nondiscriminatory way.

   • Informal and nonstandardized alternative assessment strategies are often less discriminatory because they provide information regarding the student's current skill level that is not confounded with the difficulties associated with inappropriate standardized tests.

---

**Insider Tip**

Although you need to be highly familiar with all points outlined in this section, key areas to focus on should center on RTI due to the current emphasis on this practice. Possible RTI test questions involve trend and data analysis, CBM, intervention strategies used in RTI, and determining when to refer students for special education after RTI. For formal assessments, best practice is always to use *multiple sources* of information, not just standardized testing. If you clearly understand how to interpret a WISC-IV or DAS-II, you should be able to answer most standardized testing questions so you may not have to study *all* cognitive tests; just be familiar with lesser used tests. Remember that any formal measure used should have been created or re-normed in the past 10 years.

---

## Summary and Concepts

1. Many concepts within this section may include questions regarding identifying students with particular disabilities or specific questions regarding psychological tests and their administration. Although psychometric and statistical information are typically found within *general psychological principles*, be prepared to *apply* such information regarding testing and assessments.

2. "Best practice" suggests that school psychologists *use multiple sources of information* to identify children with disabilities or problems. Although standardized cognitive assessments are central in the assessment process, such tests cannot be used in isolation. Both *formal* and *informal* measures should be used to support or supplement decisions.

3. Be highly familiar with *all aspects of RTI* and interpretation of RTI data. Know common RTI assessments such as CBM and RTI interventions. Know the difference between CBA and CBM.

4. A student's reading difficulty is the primary reason for referral to a school's RTI process. Primary interventions for reading difficulties include phonological processing training.

5. Be familiar with the major types of behavioral observational methods used in an emotional or behavioral assessment. Some common observational methods include narrative, interval, event, and ratings recording. The narrative method provides broad and narrow information from running records. Interval recording uses time-sampling techniques. Event recording documents the target behavior as it occurs.

6. Be familiar with the sources of error typically associated with behavioral assessments. For example, many behavioral surveys may have observer or rater bias. When evaluating behavioral assessments, one must study the percentage of agreement between raters. Also, observers should sample behavior more than once to increase reliability.

7. Observers during an observational assessment can be influenced by the "halo effect," fatigue, and personal biases. The previous factors are known as confounding factors.

8. Know the particular characteristics of several common behavioral and emotional assessments. Some common social and emotional assessments include the BASC, MMPI, APS, Conner's (for attention deficit hyperactivity disorder [ADHD]), and the Beck Depression Scales. A question on the Praxis Exam might ask, "Which test is used to evaluate inattention in children?" The answer in this case is the Conner's Rating Scales.

9. Know how projective measures, such as the Human Figure Drawing Test, are used. Typically, such measures are used as a supplemental part of a battery of psychological tests. Also understand the benefits and limitations of projective assessments, such as low psychometric reliability.

10. Be familiar with common adaptive and functional assessments such as the Vineland and the Adaptive Behavior Assessment System (ABAS). Most school districts suggest that standard scores (SS) on adaptive assessments *and* intelligence tests should be two standard deviations below the mean to identify children with mental retardation (SS < 70).

11. Know the steps in conducting a **functional behavioral assessment** (analysis) or FBA. The primary steps in an FBA include determining the **antecedents** of the behavior, the target **behavior** itself, and the **consequence** for the behavior. To help remember this general outline, think of A-B-C.

12. When analyzing a behavior, a psychologist should pay particular attention to the **intensity**, **frequency**, and **duration** of the behavior. The three previous characteristics of the behavior must have a significant negative impact on the student's classroom performance and/or social development in order to qualify for special education. *Note:* A student can be diagnosed with a disability, but the student may not qualify for special education services because the student is making reasonable educational progress.

13. Two main functions of a behavior are either to gain something positive or escape something negative. In addition, cognitive-behaviorists believe that attention, power and control, affiliation, and revenge are key reasons for behavior. During an FBA, one of your hypotheses may center on these motivations for behavior.

14. Although usually found within the Interventions domain, be familiar with how to use your assessment data to write an intervention plan. Remember to include positive strategies and a replacement behavior for the negative behavior in your plan. A key concept is to always link assessment to intervention.

15. Bell curve and normal curve represent normative information about typical human traits. The normal curve is based on a large population of people and reflects typical human conditions. Sixty-eight percent of people comprise the bulk (center) of the bell curve. Most standardized cognitive assessments are predicated on the normal curve theory.

16. Fluid intelligence refers to the ability to solve problems through reasoning. Fluid problem solving is not primarily based on previously learned facts,

techniques, or language. Fluid reasoning is sometimes referred to as nonverbal reasoning, immediate problem solving, or simultaneous processing. Fluid thinking involves the ability to summarize and comprehend information to solve a task.

17. Crystallized intelligence refers to the ability to solve problems by applying learned facts and language. The verbal sections of IQ tests illustrate this type of intelligence. Cattell and Horn are the chief theorists behind the fluid and crystallized intelligence model.

18. Part of a social and emotional evaluation may include aspects of emotional intelligence, which is the ability to be aware of one's emotional state, regulate one's emotions, and accurately read the emotions of others. Research in this area shows that students with low emotional and social intelligence have undesirable life outcomes.

19. Authentic and ecological assessments are an integral part of any comprehensive assessment. These types of dynamic assessments usually include observations, interviews, and having the student perform a typical classroom task, such as reading. These tasks take place in the actual environment in which the behavior is normally seen.

20. When interpreting the results of major cognitive tests, it is best practice to start at the broadest level and then narrow your interpretation to the subtest level. The most valid score is usually the full-scale score, followed by the major domain or cluster scores. Item analysis is least reliable but may reveal important information.

21. Know factors that can interfere with obtaining accurate test results. Some major factors include motivation, fatigue, undisclosed vision or hearing difficulties, and stress.

# 2

# Second Test Section: Research-Based Behavioral and Mental Health Practices

Previously, this section of the test was termed *intervention* and *prevention*. Although the name has changed, with a few exceptions, the content is largely the same. The most significant changes to this section center on more extensive concepts related to response to intervention (RTI), which was introduced in the previous chapter. Although most people associate RTI with academic intervention, it is also used for behavioral issues as well.

To prepare for this section of the test, students should have a dual approach. First, be familiar with broad interventions designed for larger groups and systems. Next, focus on intervention techniques designed for targeted (narrower) subjects, such as individual and group counseling theories and practices. For example, it is important to review individual counseling techniques such as cognitive-behavioral therapy (CBT) but also study schoolwide bully prevention strategies.

A helpful study suggestion is to segment your study notes to reflect major theories and practices under broad and narrow headings. Figure 2.1 provides an effective visual representation of how RTI can be constructed as the broader framework through which specific intervention techniques can be nested. A critical concept of RTI is the division of interventions into primary, secondary, and tertiary categories. On the Praxis™ Exam, there is a high probability that you will be asked a hypothetical question about an intervention and you must identify if the intervention is an example of a primary, secondary, or tertiary method.

Although several school psychology graduate programs typically ask students to reflect on the specific type of counseling techniques that best suits their style, students taking the Praxis Exam must be versed in several intervention theories, not just their preferred methods. Consequently, it is important to study the broad concepts from older venerable theories. Although there are many new techniques and intervention strategies, the majority of these ideas can trace their roots back to behavioral, cognitive, or developmental theories created several decades ago.

## I. Broad to Narrow: Multilevel (RTI) Model Explained

*Note:* The following examples focus on the **behavioral intervention** side of the pyramid, but RTI can focus on both academic and behavioral issues.

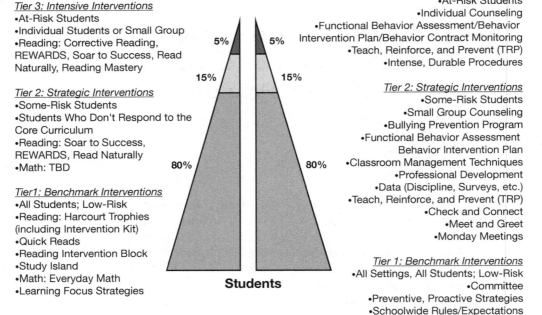

**Academic Systems**

*Tier 3: Intensive Interventions*
•At-Risk Students
•Individual Students or Small Group
•Reading: Corrective Reading, REWARDS, Soar to Success, Read Naturally, Reading Mastery

*Tier 2: Strategic Interventions*
•Some-Risk Students
•Students Who Don't Respond to the Core Curriculum
•Reading: Soar to Success, REWARDS, Read Naturally
•Math: TBD

*Tier1: Benchmark Interventions*
•All Students; Low-Risk
•Reading: Harcourt Trophies (including Intervention Kit)
•Quick Reads
•Reading Intervention Block
•Study Island
•Math: Everyday Math
•Learning Focus Strategies

**Behavioral Systems**

*Tier 3: Intensive Interventions*
•At-Risk Students
•Individual Counseling
•Functional Behavior Assessment/Behavior Intervention Plan/Behavior Contract Monitoring
•Teach, Reinforce, and Prevent (TRP)
•Intense, Durable Procedures

*Tier 2: Strategic Interventions*
•Some-Risk Students
•Small Group Counseling
•Bullying Prevention Program
•Functional Behavior Assessment Behavior Intervention Plan
•Classroom Management Techniques
•Professional Development
•Data (Discipline, Surveys, etc.)
•Teach, Reinforce, and Prevent (TRP)
•Check and Connect
•Meet and Greet
•Monday Meetings

*Tier 1: Benchmark Interventions*
•All Settings, All Students; Low-Risk
•Committee
•Preventive, Proactive Strategies
•Schoolwide Rules/Expectations
•Positive Reinforcement System
•Schoolwide Consequence System
•Schoolwide Social Skills Program
•Data (Discipline, Surveys, etc.)
•Professional Development (behavior)
•Classroom Management Techniques

5% 5% 15% 15% 80% 80%

**Students**

**FIGURE 2.1** Response to intervention model: academic and behavioral concerns.

A. **Tier 1 (Broadest Area) Primary Prevention:** This area is typically referred to as the *universal level*. This primary level involves the application of **universal interventions**.

Example of Tier 1 intervention: Positive Behavior Support (PBS) Key Ideas:

- School discipline policy is aligned with all tenets of PBS
- Five critical features of effective PBS Programs
    1. Establish and define clear and consistent schoolwide expectations.
        - Identify three to five behavioral expectations that are specific to the needs and culture within the school. Rules should be *positively* stated.
    2. Specifically teach schoolwide expectations to all students.
    3. Acknowledge students for demonstrating the expected behaviors.
    4. Develop clear and consistent consequences to respond to infractions and violations.

- The school should clearly identify consistent staff responses for behavioral infractions and should include a teaching and psychoeducational component.

5. Use objective data to evaluate schoolwide efforts.

B. **Tier 2. Strategic Interventions:** These techniques are more targeted in scope than those at the universal level, but are less so than the intensive (targeted) level.

Example of Tier 2 intervention: Bully Prevention Programs

Research indicates that approximately 20% to 30% of students are consistently involved in bullying either as victims, the bully, or both. Bullying is based on the maintenance of a chronic and purposeful power imbalance within a relationship. Although some prescriptive antibully programs are effective, it is good practice to develop a systemwide structure in a school where the *culture* does not support harassment.

**Elements of effective bully prevention programs:** (be familiar with, not necessary to memorize)

- Raise adult and student awareness. Staff commitment is critical.
- Address bystander behavior.
- Create a building-wide (systemic) process or culture to address bullying.
- Address student beliefs that support bullying; focus on decreasing victims of bullying, not necessarily eliminating bullies.
- Address student social–emotional skill deficits. Provide assertiveness training.
- Accurately assess bullying and victimization. Consider a survey to question types of victimization (e.g., rumors, physical, teasing, sexual harassment).
- Develop a specific school policy regarding bullying, especially cyberbullying.
- **Key intervention**: Increase adult monitoring on the playground, lunch areas, hallways, and other open unstructured areas.
- Improve class climate. Staff should model the skills they want their students to use.
- Zero-tolerance policies are discouraged.
- Common effective antibullying programs are Olweus Bullying Prevention and Expect Respect.
- Build basic behavioral and cognitive social skills reinforcing prosocial attitudes and behaviors and build adaptive coping strategies for social problems.

C. **Tier 3. Intensive (Targeted) Level:** Typically, this level will involve direct contact with the student who is having emotional or behavioral difficulties. Sometimes, small groups are identified where a student can receive the highest level of support or intervention.

Examples of Tier 3 intervention: *Individual counseling* that uses CBT and role playing of correct behavior; *functional behavioral assessment* (FBA) may also be employed to examine the specific antecedents, behavior, and consequences of the behavior

## II. Specific Interventions: Individual and Small Group

Interventions can take many forms. One of the most common forms of student intervention is counseling. Effective counseling is predicated upon genuine and positive rapport. The examiner needs to be versed in most of the major theories of individual counseling, ethics, and laws. In general, before individual or small-group counseling commences, the school psychologist should adhere to the following ethical principles.

A. **Ethical Principles of Counseling**

1. Obtain **parental consent** if a student is to receive ongoing services. A student can be seen before consent is acquired if **safety** is an issue.

2. Students should be informed of **confidentiality** and **exceptions** to confidentiality from the beginning of counseling sessions.

   • **Exceptions:**

   Harm to self or others

   Safety concerns

   Student request

3. Explicit **goals should be stated** and progress on goals should be observed.

B. **Major Types of Individual Counseling** and **Theories**

1. **Cognitive-Behavioral Therapy (CBT):** CBT is based on the premise that thoughts influence feelings and ultimately control behavior. CBT is one of the most highly effective interventions supported by research. Practitioners typically intervene with a student's faulty beliefs (cognition) and role play appropriate behaviors for given situations.

2. **Cognitive Therapy:** Related to reality therapy and developed by William Glasser, emphasis is on cognition and beliefs. Behavioral interventions, although important, are not the focus with this type of counseling. The psychologist tries to get the student to understand and think about the connection between behaviors and consequences.

3. **Solution-Focused Counseling:** This type of counseling incorporates CBT principles, but it is typically very brief and focused on stated outcomes.

4. **Behavioral and Behaviorism Techniques:** Behavioral interventions focus less on counseling and more on direct behavioral intervention. Behaviorism is favored by most schools because it is highly practical and forms the basis of FBA. B.F. Skinner is regarded as the father of behaviorism; he placed an emphasis on the consequence of behavior. Skinnerian approaches believe that most behavior is shaped and maintained by the consequences of the behavior.

5. **Humanistic Approach:** Developed by Abraham Maslow and Carl Rogers; believes behavioral change cannot occur without a strong positive rapport

built upon unconditional positive regard and empathy. People want to be understood by a trusted adult before they can move to change their lives.

6. **Bibliotherapy:** Bibliotherapy is a type of cognitive intervention. The therapist generally uses a student's own problem-solving skills and attempts to have the student relate to a character in a story to learn a lesson or skill that will be applicable to the student's current situation. It is important to consider a student's level of cognitive ability when implementing this type of intervention.

C. **Group Counseling:** During group counseling, a therapist can employ many of the same techniques used in individual counseling. The following are important beneficial characteristics of group counseling:

- Is time efficient
- Often found within the Tier 2 intervention level
- Promotes social learning
- Promotes skill generalization

D. **Service Learning:** Having children help or serve others is a very effective learning tool because it teaches children in an "authentic" or real-life environment. Many times, service learning teaches students social–emotional competency and empathy for those they are helping.

- **Three benefits related to service learning:**
  1. Learning is effective because students are engaged and curious about issues they experience in the real world.
  2. Students remember lessons that they learn within the community context because they are real and relevant.
  3. Service learning connects students to personal relationships and promotes pro-social actions that make a difference in people's lives.

E. **Applied Behavior Analysis (ABA) and Intervention:** This strict behavioral intervention is typically employed with autistic students. Sometimes ABA is referred to as the radical behaviorism approach due to the focus on overt behaviors.

- ABA uses systematic instruction and repeated trials to change behavior. ABA is usually highly structured and can use adult-directed strategies, as seen in Lovas training or discrete trial training.
- Systematic strategies may include incidental teaching, structured teaching, pivotal response training, functional communication training, and the picture exchange communication system (PECS).
- Discrete trial instruction (DTI) as part of ABA is a systematic way of teaching that involves a series of repeated trials to teach and maintain cognitive, behavioral, or social skills.
- Task analysis (key component of behaviorism) involves breaking down a skill into smaller steps that are easy to teach. Prompts are used to guide learners toward correct responses when teaching tasks. In the beginning, prompts are more obvious and then gradually fade away (e.g., fading

techniques). Types of prompts include physical (handover hand), gestural (pointing), modeling, and visual.

F. **Other Behavioral Interventions and Important Considerations**

Behavioral interventions should be tailored to the student's developmental and intellectual level.

- Time out can be an effective intervention if not used as a punishment. Time out or sensory breaks are effective with very young children.

- As mentioned in the previous chapter, best practice in behavioral management is to conduct an FBA on a student who has behavioral problems and modify the environment as much as possible. In short, emphasize decreasing the triggering event (antecedents) and focus on a "goodness of fit" between the student and the environment.

- When using response cost, students earn tokens based on positive classroom behavior and lose them for inappropriate behavior.

- Self-management strategies are self-directed activities that require children to monitor and/or evaluate their behavior over time. This intervention is effective with older students.

- Understand differences between the behaviorist model and the cognitive model. The behaviorist model involves the structures of the environment and provides reinforcement and punishment. Generally, behaviorism takes the position that a child learns from reinforcement and punishment. In contrast, the cognitive model is based on theories of human thinking. The child is seen as an active participant who interprets information that is received, relates it to previously acquired facts, organizes it, and stores it for later use.

- **Classwide Peer Tutoring (CWPT)** is a proactive intervention to help all students. It is similar to Vygosky's theory on collaborative learning.

  - Classwide social skills interventions should follow a modeling approach called the Tell-Show-Do-Practice-Generalize (TSDPG) approach.

## III. Special and Critical Interventions: Crisis Intervention, Prevention, and Response

A. **General Crisis Considerations**

Crisis can take many forms, from suicide to natural disasters. Psychologists must know the principles of crisis prevention, how to assess people involved in a crisis, how to manage a situation, and, finally, how to effectively follow up postcrisis.

The most effective approach to crisis-related issues is to *prevent* them from happening in the first place. Promoting school safety is a vital component in the prevention process. In the event of a crisis, the success or failure of a response to an incident depends on whether your school has a crisis team and whether the team has adequately prepared. Crisis teams are typically comprised of the administration team and other leaders, such as the school psychologist. An effective team should have practiced various drills and reviewed key crisis processes consistently and at least annually.

The following points are important for promoting a safe and responsive school environment: (These are not necessary to memorize, but be familiar with the following.)

- Adult supervision and visibility are the most essential factors of school safety.
- Conduct a formal review of all school safety policies and procedures to ensure that emerging school safety issues are adequately covered in the current school crisis plans and emergency response procedures.
- Plan a communication system that includes both school and community responders. This should also address how and where parents will be informed in the event of an emergency.
- Provide crisis training and professional development for staff based upon a needs assessment.
- Be familiar with violence prevention programs and curriculums. Teach students alternatives to violence, including peaceful conflict resolution and positive interpersonal relationship skills. Cite specific examples such as Second Step Violence Prevention, bully proofing, or other positive interventions and behavioral supports.
- Join or create a crisis or safety team and identify school needs (i.e., a needs assessment).
- Target bullying and build a peer conflict-resolution process.
- Make apparent a presence of school resource officers, local police partnerships, or security guards.
- Monitor nonstaff and school guests in your building.
- Advocate for students to take responsibility for their part in maintaining safe school environments, including student participation in safety planning. Promote compliance with school rules, reporting potential problems to school officials, and resisting peer pressure to act irresponsibly.
- Anonymous reporting systems, such as student hot lines, "suggestion" boxes, and "tell an adult" campaigns should be part of your school's culture.
- Threat-assessment and risk-assessment procedures and teams should be clearly established.
- The presence of security systems, such as video monitoring and exit door alarm systems, is sometimes useful but cannot replace adult supervision.

1. **Human Reactions to Crisis**
   - Reactions of youth to crisis or extreme stress
      - **Very young children (0 to 5 years)**: Thumb sucking, bedwetting, separation anxiety, clinging to parents, sleep disturbances, loss of appetite, fear of the dark, regression in behavior, and withdrawal from friends and routines.
      - **Elementary school children**: Fear and safety issues, aggressiveness, irritability, clinginess, nightmares, avoidance of routine activities, school problems, poor concentration, and withdrawal.

- **Adolescents:** Sleeping and eating disturbances, extreme emotions such as agitation, increase in interpersonal conflicts, somatic complaints, delinquent behavior, and poor attention or focus.
- Know key characteristics **of posttraumatic stress disorder** (PTSD). PTSD is a normal human response to extreme stress or disaster. People with PTSD have high anxiety and their reactions to stress are extreme. Obsessive thoughts about the crisis event, sleep problems, hyper-arousal, and externalizing behaviors like avoidance are common. PTSD is nested under the Anxiety Disorders in the *Diagnostic and Statistical Manual of Mental Health Disorders* (*DSM-IV-R*).

2. **Best Practice: Crisis Response Immediately Following an Event**
   - **Identify youth** who are high risk and provide support. Interventions may include individual counseling, small-group counseling, or family therapy. The school crisis response team can determine which students need supportive crisis intervention and counseling services.
   - **Support adults**, teachers, and other school staff. Provide staff members with information on the symptoms of children's stress reactions and guidance on how to handle class discussions and answer children's question. Teachers should monitor their own needs and stress reactions.
   - **Therapeutic activities** that facilitate healing postcrisis:
     - Encourage children to talk about disaster-related events. These may include a range of methods both verbal and nonverbal and incorporate varying projects (e.g., drawing, stories, and audio and video recording).
     - Reassure and normalize children's reactions and emotions.
     - Provide positive coping and problem-solving skills.
     - Strengthen children's friendship and peer support. Activities may include asking children to work cooperatively in small groups in order to enhance peer support.
     - Connect people with community resources in order to provide long-term assistance. These resource relationships need to be established with the school in advance.

3. **Additional Resources for General Crisis Intervention**
   - S. Brock, P. Lazarus, & S. Jimerson (2002). *Best Practices in School Crisis Prevention and Intervention*. Bethesda, MD: National Association of School Psychologists.
   - Natural Disasters. *NASP Resources: Helping Children and Families.* www .nasponline.org/resources/crisis_safety/naturaldisaster_teams_ho.aspx

B. **Suicide Prevention/Intervention**

Suicide is the *third* leading cause of death among youth between 10 and 19 years of age. Suicidal issues are the most serious tasks a psychologist must address. Risk factors for suicide can best be categorized as individual and environmental.

    **Individual Risk Factors**: Includes mental illness, depression, conduct disorders, substance abuse, psychological problems, and low coping skills related to a situational crisis such as death of a loved one or trauma.

**Environmental Factors:** Includes family stress, family stress or dysfunction, interpersonal conflict, and access to weapons.

- **Warning signs:**
  - Prior suicidal ideation or attempts
  - Hopelessness; student does not see a future
  - Sudden or increased involvement with alcohol and/or drugs
  - Suicidal threats in the form of direct and indirect statements
  - Suicide notes and plans
  - Preparations for final arrangements (e.g., making funeral arrangements, writing a will, giving away prized possessions)
  - Preoccupation with death
  - Changes in behavior, appearance, thoughts, or feelings

- **Protective and resiliency factors:**
  - Student feels connected to school and community
  - Student has future goals, looks forward to valued events
  - Family support and cohesion, including good communication
  - Peer support and close social networks
  - Cultural or religious beliefs that discourage suicide and promote healthy living
  - Adaptive coping and problem-solving skills, including conflict resolution
  - General life satisfaction, good self-esteem, sense of purpose

- **Best practice during high-risk situations:**
  - Get help and collaborate with colleagues.
  - Call parents or guardians and notify administration.
  - Supervise the student. It is best to always inform the student what you are going to do every step of the way. Solicit the student's assistance where appropriate. Under no circumstances should the student be allowed to leave school or be alone (even in the restroom).
  - *No-suicide contracts* have little effectiveness and are not typically recommended.
  - Instruct parents to suicide-proof the home. Whether a child is in imminent danger or not, it is recommended that both the home and school be suicide-proofed. Before the child returns home and thereafter, all guns, poisons, medications, and sharp objects must be removed or made inaccessible.
  - Call police and get consultation. All school crisis teams should have a representative from local law enforcement.
  - Document the event and provide copies to all parties. Every school district should develop a documentation form for support personnel and crisis team members to record their actions in responding to a referral of a suicidal student.

- **A Suicide Assessment and Intervention Model**

**Assessment**

- Determine whether the student has **thoughts about suicide**. (Thoughts or threats, whether direct or indirect, may indicate risk.)
- Has the student **attempted** to hurt himself before? (Previous attempts may indicate risk.)
- Does the student have **a plan** to harm himself or herself now?
- What **method** is the student planning to use and does he have access to the means? (These answers will indicate the presence of high risk.)
- What is the support system that surrounds this child? It is critical to determine the adequacy of the student's support system.
- Notify parents. **Parents must be notified**.
- Provide referrals. School districts have an obligation to suggest agencies that are nonproprietary or offer a sliding scale of fees.
- Follow up with the student and support the family.

**Suicide Postvention**

Suicide postvention is the provision of crisis intervention, support, and assistance for those affected by a completed suicide. Affected individuals may include classmates, friends, teachers, coworkers, and family members. Affected individuals are often referred to as *survivors of suicide*.

According to the American Association of Suicidology (AAS), the tasks of postvention are twofold: (1) **to reduce** the chances of anyone else committing suicide by avoiding glamorization of the deceased and (2) **to assist** staff and students with the grieving process.

It is important to be aware of cultural considerations. Attitudes toward suicidal behavior vary considerably from culture to culture.

Perhaps the greatest concern for a school psychologist after a completed suicide is **contagion**. *Contagion* is the term used to signify that one's actions might spread to others and promote more suicidal behavior, especially among teens. To avoid contagion, the school psychologist needs to advocate the following points.

**Contagion Considerations (familiarize, not memorize):**

- Avoid sensationalism of the suicide.
- Avoid glorification or vilification of the suicide victim.
- Stick to facts. Do not provide excessive details.
- The longer the delay in sharing facts, the greater the likelihood of harmful rumors.
- Avoid sharing information about the death over a school's public address system.
- Avoid schoolwide assemblies.
- Provide information simultaneously in classrooms.
- Photos of the suicide victim should *not* be used.

- "Suicide" should *not* be placed in the caption of a picture.
- Provide information to family and students about school and community resources for those people who need support.
- Staff should be provided current information regarding the death. At this time, staff needs should also be monitored.
- Provide a specific safe place for the opportunity to ask questions and express feelings.
- Emphasize the normality of grief and stress reactions.
- Identify students at risk for an imitative response.
- Do not send all students from school to funerals, stop classes for a funeral, or have moments of silence for the student.
- Do not have memorial or funeral services at school.
- Do not establish permanent memorials such as plaques. Do not dedicate yearbooks to the memory of suicide victims or dedicate songs or sporting events to the suicide victim.
- Internet resource to review on suicidal topics: www.nasponline.org/resources/crisis_safety/suicidept2_general.aspx)

C. **Loss, Death, and Grief**

Two primary challenges for the people faced with a death of a family member, well-known person, or friend are (1) processing the actual death or event and (2) coping with the loss of the loved one. The range of reactions that children display in response to the death of a significant other may be highly variable. Typical reactions include emotional shock and, at times, an apparent lack of feelings that serve to help the child detach from the pain of the moment. Regressive (immature) behaviors are frequently seen in children coping with grief. Regressive behaviors include needing to be rocked or held, difficulty separating from parents or significant others, needing to sleep in the parent's bed, or an apparent difficulty completing easy tasks. Some students have acting-out behaviors that reflect the child's internal feelings of fear, frustration, anger, loss of control, and helplessness. Finally, it is not uncommon for people to repeat themselves or ask the same questions more than once when coping with a significant loss.

- **Suggestions and Considerations About Children and Grieving**
  - Be mindful that children will be aware of the reactions of adults as they interpret and react to information about death.
  - Encourage children to talk about death or loss. Do not instruct children to deny thinking or talking about the situation.
  - Share important facts about the event and try to get a sense of what the children think about it and about death in general.
  - Note that grieving is a process, not a sole event. Children need adequate time to grieve in the manner that works for that child. Although routines may help in the healing process, do not encourage children to resume "normal" activities without the chance to deal with their emotions.

- People confronted with grief or crisis sometimes have a strong desire to "do something." Encourage children or others in the process to engage in positive activities such as bibliotherapy, writing, or making an item to mark the event.
- **Internet Resources on Grief and Emotional First Aid**
  - NASP: Helping Children Cope with Loss, Death, and Grief: Tips for Teachers and Parents. www.naspcenter.org/principals/nassp_death.html
  - National Institutes of Health (NIH): Suggestions for how to help children cope. www.nichd.nih.gov/publications/pubs/cope_with_crisis_book/sub12.cfm
  - Guidance for specific developmental levels is offered by the National Center for Child Traumatic Stress. www.nctsn.org/about-us/national-center

---

### Insider Tip

Due to the broad nature of this section's content, it will be difficult to know what to memorize. An effective approach to studying this area is to have a firm but broad understanding of research-based approaches to social–emotional assessment and interventions. Know what best practices for this content area are and let this guide your response on the Praxis Exam. In general, best practice is predicated upon having a multifactored view of assessment and a realization that people will respond differently to problems and situations. If you understand CBT, you can answer several intervention questions. Behaviorism is favored by schools, so know FBA strategies. Crisis intervention in schools is based more on humanistic principles than behaviorism. Be very clear and study suicide issues as this is a psychologist's most serious duty.

---

## Summary and Concepts

1. Be able to compare and contrast at least two primary aspects for each of the major counseling theories. Many of these theories are presented clearly in undergraduate introductory psychology texts. Your university's library should have a few undergraduate introductory textbooks. It will be well worth your time to review these major counseling theories. Although you might not be asked to *name* a specific theory or expert, you should know how to *apply* the principles of a venerable theory in a school setting.

2. Do not spend time studying nonmainstream or uncommon interventions, counseling strategies, or theories. Your time is best spent understanding well-known and widely adopted psychological interventions.

3. Person-centered humanistic counseling strives for congruence between the real and ideal self. Its aim is to actualize a person's full potential and increase

trust in oneself. Another major tenet of this theory is the belief that people naturally seek growth toward personal and universal goals if they feel they have unconditional positive regard and relationships. See concepts related to Abraham Maslow, Alfred Adler, and Carl Rogers.

4. Existential counseling helps people find their unique meaning and purpose in the world. This type of counseling increases self-awareness and stresses the importance of "choice" in tough situations. The focus is on the present and future, not the past. See Viktor Frankl's work.

5. The primary premise of Adlerian therapy is that people are motivated by social interests and by striving toward goals. Life goals drive behavior. This method emphasizes taking a person's perspective and then altering it to yield productive results.

6. Psychoanalytic counseling is Freud's theory based on early life experiences of an individual. Unconscious motives and conflicts drive behavior. The goal of this method is to make one aware of unconscious desires through interpretations. Be familiar with different Freudian stages (covered in the next chapter), but it is most likely you do not have to memorize them. It appears that the National Association of School Psychologists (NASP) is not too concerned with Freudian techniques. Rather, emphasis is placed on Freud's general contributions to the field of psychology involving the importance of early life experiences in human development.

7. In systems therapy or ecological theory, individuals are viewed as part of a larger living system. Treatment of the entire family and various other systems is important in the therapeutic change process. This approach to child support seems to be an NASP-endorsed perspective.

8. CBT is an intervention that is highly regarded and endorsed as best practice combined with FBA techniques. Be familiar with many of CBT's central principles. The CBT approach places an emphasis on a person's belief system as the cause of many problems. Internal dialogue plays a key role in behavior. Faulty assumptions and misconceptions must be addressed through talk therapy and then modified through role play or other active interventions.

9. Rational-emotive counseling was founded by Albert Ellis. This approach emphasizes confrontational techniques regarding irrational beliefs. It is not used with children in school, but it is very important to consider a person's irrational beliefs within a counseling process.

10. Gestalt therapy focuses on the wholeness and integration of thoughts, feelings, and actions. Thoughts, feelings, and actions are the three aspects of the human condition and all must be considered when helping children. In this type of therapy, it is important to move a person from an external locus of control to an internal locus of control.

11. Reality therapy centers on choices people make and how those choices are working for them. (Dr. Phil seems to use this method because he always asks his clients, "How's that working for you?") The objective is to have clients take charge of their own life by examining choices. See William Glasser's work.

12. Social skills training typically involves four processes: instruction, rehearsing, providing feedback or reinforcement, and reducing negative behaviors. Modeling and role playing are important techniques in this intervention.

13. Response cost is an effective behavioral modification method. Response cost is the removal of an earned reward that usually reduces or modifies negative behaviors. For example, a student who throws food in the cafeteria must forgo recess by cleaning up the mess. If the student is required to clean not only his food but also must help clean the entire area, this is called "overcorrection." Overcorrection is a key piece in another technique called restorative justice. Restorative practices are effective in many anti-bullying interventions.

14. Self-dialogue (self-talk) is a cognitive approach to changing behavior. It is vital to understand what a student is saying to himself before, during, and after an undesirable act. Changing self-talk can modify certain behaviors.

15. Know how to perform an **FBA**. Remember the ABCs: **A**ntecedence of the behavior, the **b**ehavior itself, and the **c**onsequence (what maintains) of the behavior. Current practice states that a focus on changing the environmental factors or triggers that cause an undesirable behavior is vital to an intervention's effectiveness.

16. Several school psychologists believe that all behavior is purposeful and is initiated by its antecedent (triggering event) and maintained by its consequences. Good interventionists always ask, "What is the payoff for the behavior?" If you change the trigger and the payoff for the target behavior, then the behavior will change.

17. A general counseling format that is commonly used in schools:
    1. Define the problem.
    2. Brainstorm ideas to address the problem.
    3. Implement the plan or modification.
    4. Evaluate the intervention's effectiveness.

18. The key elements for effective behavioral interventions are providing supportive *feedback* to the student about his behavior, giving *choices* to the student for alternative behaviors and rewards, and, finally, supplying *positive reinforcements* when expectations are met.

19. Be very familiar with how to handle general crisis issues. A thoughtful response to crisis is built upon preparation and practice. Transparency of communication about facts to impacted people is important in crisis management.

20. **Debriefing** in a crisis is a technique used to relay information and a way to flag those people who may need more mental health support. Debriefing is not a therapeutic intervention per se, although it does have some therapeutic qualities.

21. Study NASP's position and practices regarding suicide. Focus on what to do and what not to do when dealing with suicide. Also, be familiar with how to prevent suicide **contagion** issues.

22. Know how to assess for suicide and the **risk factors** associated with suicide. Know resiliency factors. Finally, know best practices of **postvention** issues.

23. Be familiar with the symptoms and the treatment of posttraumatic stress disorder (PTSD). **PTSD** is commonly associated with a crisis. Stress symptoms may not evince themselves for days, months, or years after the trauma. Symptoms in children may be masked behind inappropriate behaviors (e.g., fighting, bed wetting, and withdrawal). Psychological treatment for PTSD is similar to that of anxiety disorders. It seems like a cognitive-behavioral (C-B) approach is effective if it uses self-calming techniques, positive visualizations, and empathetic perspective taking.

24. Know the differences among primary, secondary, and tertiary intervention strategies. Remember **that prevention is a primary intervention**.

25. Be familiar with crises that are associated with violence and school shootings. There is no specific profile of school "shooters," although some general traits may exist. Bullying seems to play a central role in making some students act violently.

26. The hallmark resource that is easy to read on school violence and school shootings is published by the United States Secret Service, *Threat Assessment in Schools: A Guide to Managing Threatening Situations and Creating Safe School Climates*, May 2002. This guide can be located at the following website: www.secretservice.gov/ntac/ssi_guide.pdf

# 3

# Third Test Section: Applied Psychological Principles

This chapter covers theories of human development and behavior as well as statistical concepts as they apply to human traits (e.g., psychometrics). Although any concept discussed in this chapter might be on your version of the Praxis™ Exam, it is important to keep in mind the practical nature of school psychology. Consequently, you will most likely have questions that are more utilitarian than theoretical in nature. For example, although Freudian concepts may be helpful to know broadly, behaviorism's (B.F. Skinner's) precepts are more germane to school psychology due to their utility and popularity in schools. Focus your studying efforts on those ideas and practices that are typically employed in real practice.

In addition to pragmatic human development and learning theories, psychometric concepts should be an area of focus due to their technical nature. Although one or two simple straightforward statistical questions might be given on the Praxis Exam, most psychometric questions will be asked as part of an analysis of a hypothetical situation. Due to the previous observation, it is an effective study strategy to prepare for applied questions rather than rote memorization of particular technical constructs. In other words, when you are given an applied hypothetical question, understand *why* a response is good or not good practice.

## General Psychological Theories and Scientific Findings

### I. Human Development

A. **Piaget's Cognitive Developmental Stage Theory**. This theory is based on the premise that learning is active and children construct knowledge as they explore their environment and world.
- **Piaget's Four Stages of Development**
  1. **Sensorimotor (0 to 2 years)**: Primarily involves motor actions and senses. Children eventually come to realize that objects exist separately from them and they can manipulate objects.

2. **Preoperational (2 to 7 years):** Symbolic function emerges. Children develop the ability to make something stand for something else.

3. **Concrete Operational (7 to 11 years):** Children begin to think about more than just one dimension of a problem or situation. They gain the understanding of *conservation*. Also gain the ability to think deeper and logically.

4. **Formal Operational (11+ years):** Complex abstract thought emerges and hypothetical and deductive reasoning develops. Children perform mental operations on ideas or imagined situations.

B. **Erik Erikson's Stages of Development.** Erikson's theories are based on the notion that humans will confront a specific challenge at a given age range. Whether or not people successfully manage the challenge at a developmental stage directly impacts the positive or negative outcome.

1. **Trust versus mistrust (0 to 18 months):** Attachment to caregiver is important at this stage. A child must develop sufficient trust with the caregiver in order to explore the world. Mothers and fathers need to be warm, loving, and attentive to basic needs.

2. **Autonomy versus shame and doubt (18 months to 3 years):** Children start to develop a sense of confidence in their abilities to explore and to do things for themselves. Children begin to understand that they can control their behavior.

3. **Initiative versus guilt (3 to 5 years):** Children move from simple self-control, as in the previous stage, to taking initiative in play and in various tasks. Imaginary play and choosing activities are illustrated at this stage.

4. **Industry versus inferiority (6 to 12 years):** This stage covers the elementary school years, so know it well. Success or failure in school has lasting effects on self-efficacy and sense of adequacy. Children learn a sense of industry if they are recognized for various activities (e.g., painting, reading).

5. **Identity versus role confusion (13 to 18 years):** This stage covers the middle school and high school students. People develop a sense of identity, sense of self, and strong ego during this time. Peers, role models, and social pressures are factors associated with this stage.

6. **Intimacy versus isolation, generativity versus stagnation (or selfishness), and integrity versus despair:** The last few stages covered are important to review. However, the age ranges covered by these stages typically fall beyond the target population of school psychologists.

C. **Bandura's Social Learning Theory.** Albert Bandura's theory is a counterbalance to Skinner's strict behavioral theory of learning and development. Bandura's theory is based on children's ability to *observe* and learn vicariously. Children especially learn socially and this theory is sometimes known as social cognitive theory.

1. Humans learn not only through reward and punishment conditioning but also by observing and imitating others. Bandura observed that children exposed to the aggressive behaviors of another person were likely to imitate that behavior (e.g., bobo doll study). Although conditioning might take

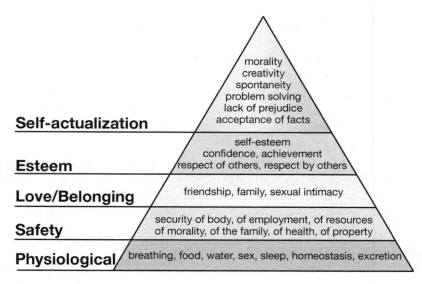

**FIGURE 3.1** Maslow's hierarchy of needs (Finkelstein, 2006).

place in some instances, in some cases no reinforcement is necessary to learn the behaviors.

2. Children imitate the behaviors of others and can select specific behaviors to imitate based on how they processed the information they observe.

D. **Maslow's Hierarchy of Needs.** Abraham Maslow, like other humanists such as Carl Rogers, offered a decidedly more positive view of human development than stage theories offered by Piaget and Freud. Maslow believed that if a student's lower level needs are supported, then higher levels in this hierarchy may be realized (see Figure 3.1).

E. **Sigmund Freud's Psychodynamic Stages**

- **Psychodynamic Theory:** A child's developing personality consists of three interrelated parts that are sometimes in conflict with each other:

  1. **Id:** Operates on the "pleasure principle." Maximizes pleasure and satisfies needs immediately.

  2. **Ego:** Is the rational, controlling part of personality that emerges and attempts to gratify needs through appropriate, socially constructive behavior.

  3. **Superego:** Emerges when the child internalizes (accepts and absorbs) parental or societal morals, values, and roles and develops a conscience.

- **Psychosexual Stages:** Changes and outcomes in the organization and interaction of the id, ego, and superego involve five discrete stages. It is believed that lack of success in any stage could result in a child developing the primary traits of the stage as an adult. Although the following stages are now considered controversial due to the lack of empirical foundation, the major contribution of Freudian theory is the emphasis on how these early experiences shape later human development.

1. **Oral (0 to 1 year):** Infant is preoccupied with activities such as eating, sucking, and biting and with objects that can be put in the mouth.

2. **Anal (2 to 3 years):** The child learns to postpone personal gratification, such as "the pleasure of expelling feces" as he is trained to use the toilet.

3. **Phallic (3 to 5 years):** The child's sexual curiosity is aroused. He or she has a preoccupation with his or her own sexual anatomy that also alerts him or her to the differences between genders. This stage is critical for forming gender identity.

4. **Latency (6 to 12 years):** Sexual drives are temporarily submerged and children avoid relationships with peers of the other gender and instead become intensely involved with peers of the same gender.

5. **Genital (12+ years):** Sexual desires reemerge and are directed toward peers.

F. **Kohlberg's Stages of Moral Development.** Kohlberg's theory is based on the level of a child's cognitive capabilities, which influence moral reasoning and behavior.

- **Kohlberg's Three Stages of Development**

  1. **Preconventional:** Behavior is based on the desire to avoid punishment and gain rewards.

  2. **Conventional:** Behavior is designed to acquire the approval of others and to maintain social relations. People accept societal regulations and conform to the rules. Children will conform to what parents say is right or wrong solely based on conforming and not consider any ethical standards.

  3. **Postconventional:** Judgments on right and wrong are logical and conduct is controlled by an internalized ethical code that is relatively independent of the approval or disapproval of others.

G. **B. F. Skinner's Behaviorism.** Behaviorism has been covered in the previous chapters and should be referenced throughout this guide. As mentioned, Skinner believed that human behavior is largely shaped by the environment and through the consequences that immediately follow a behavior. Although Behaviorism is a major theory of human development, it is narrow and simplistic in scope. A criticism of strict behaviorism is that it does not consider the cognitive aspects of humans or the neurobiological features of behavior.

## II. Common Disorders: Child and Adolescent Psychopathology

The reader should review developmental disabilities typically associated with special education. Be able to *recognize* hallmark traits, etiology, and prevalence rates for various disabilities. For example, know the traits associated with autism and pervasive developmental disability (PDD), Asperger syndrome, Fragile X syndrome, Down syndrome, mental retardation, bipolar disorder, and attention deficit hyperactivity disorder (ADHD). Of particular consideration, know the nature and treatments associated with posttraumatic stress disorder (PTSD) as this disorder is commonly diagnosed in people after exposure to a crisis. On the Praxis Exam, crisis scenario questions are common, so be prepared to apply your knowledge.

*Important Note:* For the diagnosis of a true disorder, the problem must significantly impede general life functioning. In school systems, a lesser level is required to qualify a student for special education, so the term *identification* is used instead of the term *disorder*. In the latter case, to be formally identified for an individual education plan (IEP), one *must* have educational or severe social impact, not just a diagnosis of a clinical disorder. It is a good idea for school psychologists to be aware of the differences between identification of a disability for school purposes and clinical disorders outlined by the *Diagnostic and Statistical Manual of Mental Disorders* (*DSM-IV-TR* and *DSM-5*).

- **Attention Deficit Hyperactivity Disorder (ADHD):** ADHD is considered one of the most prevalent disorders seen in schools and usually co-occurs with other problems such as learning disabilities. In large schools, typically 3% to 7% of the population will be diagnosed with ADHD. The disorder impacts boys more than girls with a 3:1 ratio commonly cited. Hallmark traits of ADHD could include impulsivity, inability to sustain attention, constant movement, and lack of self-regulation. ADHD may be combined type or predominately hyperactivity. ADHD may have genetic roots. Dopamine and neuroepinephrine deficiency causing prefrontal lobe brain dysfunction is implicated in this disorder. ADHD is largely responsive to medication treatments. Prenatal nicotine or other drug usage by the mother may be risk factors.

- **Anxiety:** Anxiety is common disorder in society, typically with 3% to 5% prevalence rate and a 2:1 ratio in favor of females. Anxiety disorder may have genetic links in some cases. It can be generalized or specific (e.g., phobias). Humans have psychological vulnerability to highly stressful or chronic stress events. PTSD is a common stress reaction to a crisis.

- **Posttraumatic Stress Disorder (PTSD):** is a subset of anxiety disorder. PTSD is a common and persistent extreme reaction to very stressful or traumatic events. People with PTSD have recurrent nightmares, hypersensitivity to environmental triggers, avoidant behaviors, and constant recounting of the stressful situation.

- **Depression:** Like anxiety, major depressive disorder has a high prevalence rate, with stated figures for males of 3% to 5% and 8% to 10% for females. Depression may have genetic links, but it also has strong situational and environmental causes. Medication is effective in many cases. Depression treatment using a combined approach of therapy and medication is most effective.

- **Bipolar Disorder**: This disorder has biological underpinnings that create large mood fluctuations from depression to mania. Underactivation in the left temporal brain lobe has some research support as the cause of this disorder. It is generally responsive to a combination of counseling and medication.

- **Conduct Disorder (CD) and Oppositional Defiant Disorder (ODD):** Although some research indicates that CD may have some genetic or biological influences, school systems generally regard CD as a behavioral disorder that is mostly the result of interactions between environment and individual, inadequate parenting, peer rejection, academic failure, poverty, or low cognitive abilities. A student's skill deficits related to subpar coping is also a contributing factor for CD. For the purpose of an IEP, qualification may not include CD or ODD due to the belief that this disorder has a volitional choice component.

- **Autism and Pervasive Developmental Disability (PDD):** PDD spectrum disorders impact more males than females; there is a relatively low incidence of this disorder. Prevalence rates for autism spectrum disorders used to range from 1 in every 2,500 people but now are stated to be 1 in 88. Controversy surrounds the previous figure due to changes in diagnosing the disorder and whether Asperger syndrome is counted as autism. Asperger syndrome rates are higher than those rates for autism. Behavior modification, "shaping," and direct hands-on teaching with pictures are common interventions for children with autism. Also, the use of toys, increased structure, motor imitation, and family participation are useful methods of intervention. Currently, there is no cure for autism. Genetics and brain abnormalities are implicated in the cause.

- **Down Syndrome (Trisomy 21):** Down syndrome impacts 1 out of 700 to 800 people. The disorder is believed to be caused by an extra chromosome (chromosomal disorder). Most children with this disorder also have mental retardation. Interventions associated with this disorder include hands-on learning, tight structure in the classroom, visual communication systems, and social skills training. There is no cure for Down syndrome.

- **Tourette Syndrome:** Tourette syndrome is a tic disorder with a possible genetic component that can be evinced by extremely stressful events or a virus in the brain. Relaxation, social skills training, medication, and cognitive-behavioral interventions are widely used with this disorder. This disorder may involve involuntary twitching and facial expression or verbal outbursts. Tics may become more apparent after the use of stimulant medication to treat a co-occurring problem like ADHD and anxiety disorder.

- **Mental Retardation (MR):** Diagnosed by standardized IQ test scores that are given in a standard deviation of 15 points, children with MR have very low cognitive abilities and life skills. A standard score (SS) ranging from 55 to 69 is considered mild retardation, SS from 40 to 54 is moderate, and below 40 is severe. A student must perform significantly low on adaptive and functional life skills measures such as the Vineland or ABAS to receive this diagnosis.

  *Note:* Significant limited intellectual capacity (SLIC) is an equivalent of the term *mental retardation.* This identification changed in 2012 to the term **intellectual disability (ID).** Children who have SLIC must have standard IQ scores at least 2 standard deviations below the mean (SS < 70) *and* adaptive skills, as measured by standardized surveys, also below 70.

- **Significant Identifiable Emotional Disability (SIED):** As with learning disabilities (LDs), schools use SIED as an umbrella term that captures anxiety disorders, depression, and psychoses. The key to this disability is that children must be impacted in various settings, and one of these settings must be school. Emotional disturbances cannot be due to situational factors, and interventions must have been attempted.

  *Note:* This term is changing to **significant emotional disability (SED).** A school identification of SED will emphasize a child's emotional disability and will generally not be based on conduct disorder or chronic willful behaviors.

- **Speech and Language Disabilities:** Children with these disabilities have difficulty with expressive and/or receptive language. Oral motor dysfunctions result in speech difficulties. Language disorders are broadly situated in the left hemisphere of the brain. Although different states use various standards to qualify for language disorders, qualifying language tests typically have scores that fall below the ninth percentile. Common speech–language assessments are the Clinical Evaluation of Language Fundamentals (CELF) and Peabody tests.

- **Dyslexia:** Dyslexia is a diagnostic term for reading disorders. Schools rarely use this term on an IEP and instead use "reading difficulties." Most reading problems are linked to phonological processing dysfunction. However, there is a minority of children whose reading problems are tied to visual processing problems. Proper assessment of dyslexia involves assessment of phonological processes (e.g., phonemic awareness, segmentation, and sound deletion). Simple word-rate reading is an effective evaluation tool.

  *Note:* Reading difficulties are the most common reason for special education and RTI referrals. Although phonological training and direct reading instruction are highly effective interventions, students with both phonological processing difficulties and fluency deficits are resistant to remediation.

- **Dyscalculia:** This is a diagnostic term for mathematical disorders. Students with mathematical or quantitative reasoning difficulties have a prevalence rate of 2% to 5% within the population, but this figure might be a low estimate. Tests frequently employed to discern a dyscalculia are the Key Math Test and spatial and working memory subtests from various cognitive abilities tests.

- **Specific Learning Disability (SLD):** SLD is a practical term schools use to capture various learning problems such as dyslexia, dyscalculia, or spelling disorders.

## Other Important Terms Related to School Difficulties

- **English as a Second Language (ESL):** Foreign students are typically placed in ESL classes in schools because they do not fully understand the English language. It seems the National Association of School Psychologists (NASP) desires ESL students be provided education in *both* languages. Full immersion or instruction only within a child's native language is generally not supported.

- **Readiness:** This term is used to denote a student's biological and physiological maturational level to enter school (usually kindergarten).

- **Learned Helplessness:** This term was coined by Martin Seligman. Learned helplessness describes a behavior that results from the belief that one cannot control the events in one's environment. People with a learned helplessness belief are prone to depression, fatalistic perspectives, low self-esteem, and low achievement. People believe events that happen to them have an external, not an internal, orientation. In short, life happens to them with little control.

- **Theory of the Mind:** Theory of mind is when a person begins to understand that other people have their own private thoughts, perspectives, and feelings. This theory is associated with autism.

## III. Theories and Concepts Related to Learning and Intelligence

This section might encapsulate concepts previously discussed because learning can be construed as behavior, which we have covered in previous sections. Schools typically use behavioristic techniques to teach students or shape their behaviors.

A. **Key Terms and Concepts Related to Human Learning**

1. **Premack Principle**: This principle was developed by David Premack. In short, this theory offers that a lower level behavior can be shaped by a higher level behavior. For example, a student is not allowed to play outside unless he does his homework first. This theory is sometimes termed *contingency* learning because a desired behavior is contingent on first completing a lesser desired behavior.

2. **Immediacy**: This is a key behaviorism concept. Consequences (e.g., rewards) should occur immediately after the behavior in order to be an effective reinforcement.

3. **Negative Reinforcement**: This is often confused with punishment. Unlike punishment, a behavior *increases* under negative reinforcement. A stimulus is removed, which causes a behavior to increase.

4. **Positive Reinforcement**: A behavior occurs, a rewarding stimulus is provided, and the behavior *increases*.

5. **Fixed Ratio Reinforcement**: A specific number of behaviors must occur before a reinforcer is given.

6. **Variable Ratio**: The number of behaviors needed in order to receive the reinforcer varies. Variable schedules of reinforcement, once a behavior is established by this method, are *resistant to change*.

7. **Frequency, Duration, and Intensity**: These vital aspects of behavior are measurable and are key parts in all behavior modification plans for students.

8. **Shaping**: Shaping is a technique that creates a behavior by reinforcing approximations of the desired target behavior.

9. **Extinction**: Eliminating the reinforcers or rewards for the behavior terminates the problem behavior.

B. **Theories of Intelligence**

Intelligence is a difficult term to defined. Despite some controversy involving the definition and how to assess the construct of intelligence, it can be construed as one's ability to think rationally and act purposefully. Intelligence can also be conceptualized as a person's ability to learn effectively and efficiently. Generally, intelligence is how one *applies* knowledge to problem solving.

Intelligence shares some variance with wisdom and learned skills, but it is conceptually different. There are several factors that support intelligent behavior such as memory, attention, and processing speed. It is generally assumed that intelligence is solely a brain-based function and it directly impacts a child's ability to learn and achieve in school. School psychologists employ cognitive tests to determine whether a student has the ability to attain academic standards (e.g., set expectations) and to help to craft intervention strategies. *The current endorsement by NASP is that cognitive test results need to be tied to interventions.*

1. **Spearman's Theory of Intelligence: Two-Factor Theory of Intelligence:** Charles Spearman is a prominent figure in intelligence test theory. He is cited as creating the modern statistical foundation for intelligence tests. Spearman primarily believed in a general intelligence factor known as "g." Spearman's "g" is seen in overall or full-scale IQ scores. Specific factors are correlated with specific abilities.

2. **Thurstone's Primary Mental Abilities:** Louis Thurstone held a somewhat opposite view from Spearman, but he is equally influential in the field of psychometrics. He claimed there were at least 11 primary mental abilities. Spearman believed these abilities and dimensions were causal properties of behavior and he did not view intelligence as a unitary construct like "g."

3. **Cattell–Horn–Carroll (CHC) Theory of Cognitive Abilities:** The CHC theory of intelligence is *a highly regarded and widely adopted theory used to construct most major cognitive abilities tests* such as the WISC-IV, DAS-II, and WCJ Test of Cognitive Abilities. CHC is steeply anchored to well-established statistical techniques. Although subcomponents of the theory are given, it may *not be necessary to memorize terms like Gf, but do understand the implications of the parts that make up the CHC theory.*

   **Components of CHC Theory (Statistically Derived)**

   - **Gf:** Usually called fluid intelligence or fluid reasoning, this refers to inductive and deductive reasoning with materials and processes that are new to the person doing the reasoning.

   - **Gc:** Usually called crystallized ability or crystallized verbal ability, this refers to the application of acquired knowledge and learned skills to answering questions and solving problems that present broadly familiar materials and processes.

   - **Gv:** This involves a range of visual processes, ranging from fairly simple visual perceptual tasks to higher level visual and cognitive processes.

   - **Ga:** This is auditory processing, such as recognizing similarities and differences between sounds and recognizing degraded spoken words, such as words with sounds omitted or separated.

   - **Gs:** Also called processing speed, this refers to measures of clerical speed and accuracy.

   - **Gsm:** This refers to short-term or immediate memory.

   - **Glr:** This involves memory storage and retrieval over longer periods.

4. **Das-Naglieri PASS Model:** This model of the *brain function* functionally divided the brain into four units and was originally proposed by A. E. Luria. This theory holds significant promise to help practitioners to conceptualize intelligence as it relates to brain function.

**Four Functional Units of Brain Processes (PASS)**

1. Planning
2. Attention
3. Simultaneous Processing
4. Successive Processing

## IV. Language Development

### A. Key Terms and Concepts Related to Language Development

1. **Phonology:** System of sounds that a language uses. Note that people commonly confuse phonemic awareness with phonological processing. Phonemic awareness is a component of the broader construct phonological processing.

2. **Phoneme:** The basic unit of a language's *sound* or phonetic system. It is the smallest sound units that affect meaning. Example: /s/.

3. **Morpheme**: Language's smallest units of *meaning*, such as prefix, suffix, or root word. Example: "pre" in the word "preheat."

4. **Semantics:** The study of *word meanings* and combinations, such as in phrases, clauses, and sentences.

5. **Syntax:** Prescribes *how* words may combine into phrases, clauses, and sentences.

6. **Pragmatics:** A set of rules that specify appropriate language for particular social contexts.

   *Note:* Acquiring two languages, simultaneously, as a child can sometimes slow language development. Some children will have difficulty with "code switching."

### B. Language Acquisition Device (LAD)

**Noam Chomsky** is a key person to study as he is widely known as an expert on language development. He proposed that children are born with an innate mental structure that guides their acquisition of language and grammar. Chomsky also asserted that certain "universal features" that are common to all languages are innate (e.g., subject, verb, object). Perhaps Chomsky is best known for the concept of a *critical period* for language and LAD.

   Chomsky's views about language development center on the *interactionist view*. The interactionist perspective states that language is learned in the context of spoken language but assumes as well that humans are in some way biologically prepared for learning to speak. Language interactions involve the interplay between a child's biology and social environment.

### C. Brain Areas Involved in Language

The left hemisphere of the cerebral cortex plays a primary role in language.

1. **Broca's Area:** Located in the frontal portion of the left hemisphere, this brain area supports grammatical processing and *expressive* language production.

2. **Wernicke's Area:** Located in the medial temporal lobe, this section of the brain supports word-meaning comprehension and *receptive language.*

## V. Test Measurement and Statistical Concepts

*Note:* For most measurements or statistical questions on the Praxis Exam, you will most likely be asked how to interpret assessment results rather than calculate complex psychometrics. If you have to calculate a metric on the exam, it will probably be simple statistics such as the range, mode, mean, or median from a set of scores.

A. **Types of Tests, Evaluations, and Assessments**

1. **Cognitive Abilities Tests:** Examples of cognitive abilities tests include the WISC-IV and DAS-II. These tests are sometimes referred to as IQ or aptitude tests. Cognitive tests are used as a way to *predict future learning* and are normally norm referenced. Selection and placement decisions typically involve predictions about future learning or performance based on the present characteristics of an individual. Despite some controversy with cognitive tests, they remain a primary scientific resource to explain why students have difficulty learning.

2. **Formative Evaluations:** There are specific assessments used to determine a student's strengths and weaknesses. Formative evaluations typically evaluate the academic areas where students are doing well and those areas they are doing poorly. The results are used to guide and inform future instruction.

3. **Summative Evaluations:** These provide a review and summary of a person's accomplishments to date. These evaluations are generally provided at the end of a grading period to provide a summary of student achievement.

4. **Achievement Tests:** A type of performance test that describes the skills a person has learned in school. Achievement tests are concerned with the mastery of a type of skill such as reading, writing, and math. These can be a formal and norm-referenced like cognitive tests. Well-known tests of achievement include the Woodcock-Johnson Test of Achievement and Wechsler Achievement Test.

5. **Domain-Referenced and Criterion-Referenced Tests:** These are tests concerned with the level mastery of a defined skill set. Their purpose is solely on reaching a standard of performance on a specific skill. The test itself and the domain of content it represents provide the standard. These are not norm-referenced or standardized.

6. **Norm-Referenced Tests:** In these tests performance is evaluated not in relation to the set of tasks but in relation to the performance of a more general reference group. The quality of performance is defined by comparison with the behavior of others. Scores are described in terms of how far a student is from the mean (average) of a group. Scores fall on a normal curve of scores.

B. **Types of Test Scores and Norms**

1. **Percentile Ranks:** A percentile rank indicates the percentage of people surpassed by an individual on a standardized test. An example is a student with a score in the 33rd percentile who has scored better than 33% of

those who took the same test. Although most people understand percentile ranks, *the major problem with this metric is that it is not an equal-interval measurement.*

2. **Grade Norms and Equivalents:** Students are matched to grade groups whose performance they equal. Average scores are obtained from individuals in a grade and compared with the grade group that their performance matches. An example is a student with a grade equivalent of 3.5, which means the student is performing as an average child in the fifth month of her third-grade year. **Caution** should be used, as grade equivalents are very poor metrics.

3. **Age Norms and Equivalents:** Age equivalents (AE) are similar to grade equivalents. An individual is matched to the age equivalent whose performance he or she equals. AE is the average score earned by individuals at a specific age. *As with other unequal interval metrics, this type of score should be used with a high degree of caution.*

4. **Standard Scores:** Standard scores are psychometrically sound measures and are used to describe a person's position within the normal curve of human traits. These scores express the relative position of a score as the average (mean) of other scores. Standard scores use standard deviations in their formulas. *Most psychologists are encouraged to use standard scores when possible.*

C. **Basic Statistical Terms Used in Descriptions of the Normal (Bell) Curve**

- **Range:** The difference between the highest and lowest score within an entire set of scores.

- **Median:** The middle score in a set of scores wherein 50% of scores fall on either side of the middle score.

- **Mode:** The most frequently occurring score in a set of scores.

- **Mean:** The average score of a set of scores. The mean is found by adding all the scores in a set together and dividing by the total number of scores. This is regarded as one of the best measures of central tendency.

- **Variance:** A measure of how far a set of numbers is spread out.

- **Standard Deviation:** A measure of the spread of a set of values from the mean value. The standard deviation is the square root of the variance. It is a measure of dispersion. Standard deviation (SD) is used as a measure of the spread or scatter of a group of scores as a way to express the relative position of a single score in a distribution. It is the square root of the average of the squared deviations from the mean.

- **Z-scores:** Z-scores have a mean of zero and a standard deviation of one. They are not used much in education or education reports.

- **T-scores:** T-scores have a mean of 50 and a standard deviation of 10.

- **Stanines:** A standard nine-point scale (stanine) is a standard score used with educational tests. Stanines (also used within normal distributions like Z- and T-scores) have a mean of five, and each stanine unit represents one half of a standard deviation (see Figure 3.2).

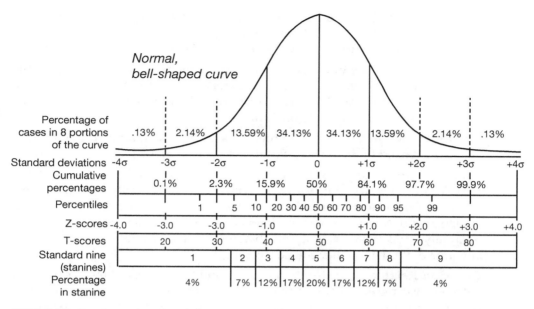

**FIGURE 3.2** Psychometric and statistical comparison chart.

## D. Reliability and Validity of Measurement (for Formal Standardized Tests)

1. **Reliability:** Reliability refers to standardized tests and scores that are *consistent and stable across time*. Test reliability is crucial for effective assessment of a student's functioning as it relates to cognition, academic skills, and emotional development.

- **Reliability Coefficient:** This statistic illustrates the *consistency* of a score or the *stability* of a score. An appropriate reliability coefficient for standardized tests should generally be around or above $r = .80$. The higher the reliability coefficient the better.

- **Standard Error of Measurement (SEM):** This metric is an estimate of error used when interpreting an individual's test score. With every test there are errors due to a host of factors. Tests results rarely provide the "true score" due to error. SEM plays a pivotal role in calculating reliability. *Note:* It is doubtful you will have to actually calculate SEM or other complex psychometrics on the Praxis Exam.

- **Methods to Assess Reliability:**
  - **Test–Retest:** Testing a person with the same test twice. The two scores are then correlated together using statistical methods. Theoretically, both scores should be highly similar if the test is reliable. A 2-week time interval between re-taking the test is the minimal time frame recommended.
  - **Alternate and Parallel Forms:** Alternate forms of a test should be thought of as two tests built according to the same specifications but composed of separate samples from the defined behavior domain. They must take into account variation resulting from tasks and correlation between two test forms to provide the reliability coefficient.

- **Split Half**: Take a full test and create two tests from it, being careful to share difficult and easy items on both tests. Both tests are administered, even on the same day, and the scores on both tests are correlated.
- **Internal Consistency Reliability**: An estimate of the reliability of the total test is developed from an analysis of the statistics of the individual test items. Each test item is compared to the total set of items. This statistic is express in terms of Cronbach's alpha.
- **Interrater Reliability:** The reliability of people administrating the test is increased by increasing the number of raters or judges.

2. **Validity:** Like reliability, validity is vital to a test's effectiveness and usefulness. Validity regards the degree to which the test actually measures what it claims it measures. To put it another way, validity is the degree to which evidence and theory support the interpretation of test scores. As stated with reliability coefficients, validity coefficients are acceptable if they are generally above .80. The higher the coefficient, the better.

**Criterion-Related Validity:** Criterion validity concerns the correlation between two measures (tests) that are designed to measure human traits. If two tests measure the same trait, the correlation between the tests should obviously be higher. If one of the two tests is not designed to measure the same trait, the correlation should be lower between the two tests.

- **Face and Content Validity**: This involves how rational and reasonable the test and test items look. During test construction, experts in the area being examined are asked to evaluate whether test items look logical. For example, a math test would be considered invalid if all test items asked about cats.
- **Convergent Validity**: Convergent validity is determined when a test is correlated with another test that has a similar purpose and measure the same trait. For example, if a test that measures ADHD correlates highly or "converges" with another well-known test of ADHD, then the test is said to have good validity.
- **Divergent Validity**: Divergent validity is established by correlating two tests that measure two different traits. For example, a test that measures ADHD should have a low correlation to a test that measures depression. However, there might be a low correlation between the two traits being measured.

**Construct-Related Validity**: This refers to whether a trait or construct is being measured.

- **Predictive Validity**: A valid test should have high predictive value. For example, a valid test of cognitive ability should be able to predict a student's achievement in school. A student with a standard score of 75 on a cognitive test is predicted to struggle in school and to perform below grade level.
- **Discriminant Validity**: A valid test should be able to discriminate between students who have the trait being measured and those who do

not have the trait. For example, a student scoring high on an anxiety measure could be identified with an anxiety disorder from those students who do not have an anxiety disorder.

3. **Confounding Factors That May Influence Test Reliability and Validity**
   - Motivation and lack of effort when taking the test
   - Personal issues, such as lack of sleep, fatigue, or test anxiety
   - Language difficulty or not understanding directions
   - Environmental factors, such as noise, lights, and distractions
   - Values and beliefs of the test taker
   - Racial bias
   - Socioeconomic status (SES) of the test taker
   - Family dynamics
   - Mental health issues

4. **Additional Testing Considerations and Terms**
   - If a standardized test is administered with the use of an interpreter and the test is not normed on the special population related to the student being tested, this will have a profound impact on the results reliability and validity. *Note:* **NASP does not encourage the use of standardized tests with interpreters if the test is not appropriately normed.** There is a chance that a test item on the Praxis Exam will be related to this previous point. Understand the difficulties testing ESL students.

   - **False Positives**: A student performs well on a test, but in actuality, the student is failing in the authentic environment. For example, a student scores high on a reading comprehension test but has difficulty reading in class.

   - **False Negatives**: A student performs poorly on a test, but in actuality, the student is making acceptable progress in the authentic environment with little or no problem.

---

## Insider Tip

Studying for the general psychological section is difficult due to its broadness. As with other sections, focus your efforts on the practical aspects of school psychology. For example, few school psychologists employ Freudian theory; instead, they prefer an eclectic approach primarily based on CBT. Generally, know the broad benefits of the most widely used theories. Piaget, Skinner, Maslow, and Bandura are widely accepted theorists who most school psychologists endorse. In regard to testing and psychometrics, I have not heard of any test taker having to use statistical formulas to solve test items. Psychometric test questions mostly center on why a test or test interpretation is appropriate or not. Again, most test questions appear to involve the application of knowledge, not the memorization of specific facts.

# Summary and Concepts

## General Psychological Theories and Principles

1. **Learned helplessness:** A sense of hopelessness and depression that develops from a pattern of failures. See Martin Seligman's work with dogs.

2. **External locus of control** is the belief that events happen to you. Success is attributed to "luck." **Internal locus of control** is the belief that one's effort and skills control one's future. Obviously, successful students believe in an internal locus of control.

3. **Behaviorism** focuses on environmental factors and reinforcement of behaviors. Behavioristic interventions and experiments are strongly empirically driven and focus on strict data collection for scientific proof of effectiveness. Schools favor this theoretical orientation to manage or change behaviors.

4. Behaviorists use the **Premack Principle** to modify behavior. This principle emphasizes that a desirable task can reinforce a lower level task. For example, a child may eat a cookie (higher level task) after she finishes homework (lower level task).

5. **Social learning theory** states that people learn not only through reinforcers and punishers (i.e., B.F. Skinner's behaviorism) but also through observation. Albert Bandura illustrated that children can act aggressively by merely watching the violent behavior of others. The keyword to remember for Bandura's research is "modeling."

6. Be familiar with **Kohlberg's stages of moral development:** (1) the preconventional stage is usually for children in whom behavior is motivated by avoidance of punishments; (2) the conventional stage is where most people are situated—it focuses on conformity to social norms and approval of others; and (3) the postconventional stage centers on high ethics and moral principles of conscience (i.e., personal principles, not just laws of society).

7. Be familiar with **Piaget's theories:** Sensorimotor, Preoperational, Concrete, and Formal. According to Piaget, human development is the progressive adaptation to the environment through *assimilation and accommodation*. Infants are biologically predisposed to develop and acquire information by interacting with their environment. For example, a child who thinks a dime is worth less than a nickel because it is physically smaller soon learns through play or "pretend" spending that it is actually worth more.

8. Be familiar with **Erik Erikson's psychosocial stages** as they relate to school aged children: trust versus mistrust, autonomy versus shame, initiative versus guilt, industry versus inferiority, and identity versus role confusion.

9. Freudian or psychoanalytic theory may be on some tests, but my research has not revealed that this area is the basis for more than just one or two questions. It seems Freud's contributions to school psychology are broad in nature. Instead of memorizing his stages of development, I would be familiar with the Freudian concepts that are not controversial and are practical in nature. For example, Freud was one of the first psychologists to realize the importance

of "critical periods" and the significance of early experiences. Be familiar with how the id, ego, and superego interact.

10. Review developmental disabilities typically associated with special education. Be able to recognize hallmark traits for various disabilities. For example, know the major traits associated with autism, PDD, Asperger syndrome, Fragile X syndrome, Down syndrome, mental retardation, bipolar disorder, and ADHD.

## Test, Measurement, and Statistical Concepts

1. Most common cognitive assessments have a mean (average) of 100 and a standard deviation of 15 points. Therefore, if a student scores 118 on a cognitive test, that student is said to be slightly *over* 1 standard deviation above the mean (above average).

2. Watch for tricky questions regarding standard deviations. Remember that a standard score of 100 is average, not 50. A standard score of 50 is considerably far below average. However, a score that is in the 50th percentile (not percentage) is equal to a standard score of 100.

3. Some questions might ask you to compare scores, so understand how to interpret standard scores based on the interpretative range in which the scores fall.

4. **Ipsative scores** examine a pattern of scores within an individual to determine relative (to self) strengths and weakness. Ipsative scores compare scores on a test to the test taker rather than to a group.

5. **Criterion measurement** is *not* based on the bell curve (normal curve) population or group, but it is based on a specific criteria or content to be mastered. Criterion measurement is typically used in self-paced studies and in response to intervention (RTI) processes.

6. Remember it is best practice to give the range of scores that a test score falls within due to the standard error of measurement (SEM). The SEM is used to develop confidence brackets (intervals or bandwidths) around a score on a standardized test and the confidence interval should be reported.

7. T-scores have a mean of 50 and a standard deviation of 10. For example, a T-score of 65 would be above average and 1.5 standard deviations above the mean. It is important not to confuse T-scores with standard scores.

8. A percentile is the percentage of people who score at or below the percentile score given on a test. Percentiles use percentages but are not percentages themselves. It is very important to understand that percentile, like some other metrics, is not equal interval statistics. Consequently, unequal interval statistics tend to exaggerate score differences the farther from the mean the scores get.

9. The reason professionals prefer to use standard scores is because they are "equal interval" scores, whereas other types of scores are not equal in their measurements of central tendency.

10. The effect size is a statistic that illustrates the overall effect of an intervention based on comparing the average (mean) performance of two groups. An

effect size of .50 or more is typically considered large, .30 is moderate, and .10 is small.

11. Standardized testing follows very strict rules for administration, scoring, and interpretation. Such tests have verifiable statistical properties associated with the test's validity and reliability. The chief benefit of standardized tests is that it compares a person to what is expected of a large population and reveals what is *normal* performance for a given trait or skill.

12. Reliability is a vital characteristic for standardized tests. Reliability is the ability of a test to produce similar results over time. IQ test results remain somewhat stable (reliable) across time.

13. Validity is another highly important test characteristic of all standardized tests. Validity is a test's ability to measure what it purports to measure. For example, a reading test measures the ability to read, not to solve math problems.

14. Be familiar with the different types of validity such as predictive, convergent, discriminative, and divergent validity. Typically, common standardized tests use convergent validity to support their use. An example of convergent validity is when a new test is correlated with an established test. If the new test has validity; it should have a high correlation with the established test. Also, a test can be highly reliable but not necessarily valid.

15. A type I error is when you state that your test results are true, but in actuality they are not true (rejecting a null hypothesis). A type II error is stating something is false, but it is really true (accepting a null hypothesis).

16. Correlation is an association or relationship among variables. For example, research has shown a high correlation between smoking and lung cancer. However, remember that a strong correlation does not mean one variable *causes* another variable to change. Correlations above .80 are said to be strong and desirable for test purposes. Correlations are useful in predicting events. For example, IQ tests are useful in predicting a student's future grades. This is why when a child has a high IQ but low achievement (grades), it is believed that something is interfering with that child's learning.

17. To raise the "power" of an experiment or test, you must increase the number and types of participants. Raising the power makes your experiment or test more reliable and valid. Typically, the number of subjects ($N$) starts to approximate bell curve characteristics at 50. The higher the $N$, the better.

# 4

# Fourth Test Section: Research-Based Academic and Classroom Practices

School psychologists are expected to be experts in every type of human behavior, especially those behaviors that pertain to learning. For the Praxis™ Exam, be familiar with learning theories and current instructional practices. Learning is an intimate and personal process, and psychologists are keenly aware of the individual differences (styles) of how students acquire knowledge. Although teachers also understand the benefits of individualized instruction, in practice, teachers have great difficulty tailoring instruction for each student's learning style. There are myriad reasons why students struggle to learn, ranging from differences in cognitive abilities, to emotional problems, to family dynamics. Psychologists may be called upon by school staff for assistance with teaching students, especially those with disabilities.

## *Effective Pedagogy and Instruction*

A. **Basic Principles of Effective Instructions**
1. Activate a student's *prior knowledge* before teaching.
2. Make *connections* between new learning and a student's current knowledge. Make learning relevant to the student's life.
3. Do not overload students' abilities when teaching new concepts, especially their working memory. Working memory capacity is typically limited to four to seven bits of information.
4. Provide the optimum level of instruction, not too hard and not too easy. Have student experience some success and some challenge. This concept is related to the *Zone of Proximal Development*.
5. *Model* desired responses, have explicit expectations, and provide exemplars of completed work.
6. Allow time for practice. Provide *corrective feedback in frequent practice* of skills. Have cognitive rest periods (days) between teaching new concepts.

7. Feedback needs to be provided in an *immediate* and positive manner.

8. *Multimodal* teaching is good practice. Incorporate "learning by doing" when possible. Use visual, auditory, and kinesthetic modalities.

9. Student learning develops as target skills progress through phases: Acquisition → proficiency → generalization → adaptation.

B. **Specific Instructional Strategies**

1. A good general model to follow when teaching is to have an **explicit and systematic approach** to presenting information. For example, students are told specifically *what* they are learning before their lesson starts every class period. Next, students are told *why* they need to learn the concept. Third, the teacher models the new skill or concept. After new information is presented, students will practice with teacher feedback. Finally the students practice the skill alone. Explicit instruction also includes breaking down tasks or new concepts into small manageable steps. *The steps to learning involve the "I do, we do, you do" approach.*

2. **Differentiated instruction** is critical when teaching groups. It requires educators to respond to the *individualized needs and abilities* of all learners within the regular education environment.

3. **Small-group instruction** allows the teacher to monitor student mastery of educational concepts, provide instant feedback, and accommodate individual learning needs.

4. **Cooperative learning**, proffered by the famous theorist Vygosky, is a proven teaching technique. Students work collaboratively to learn new concepts. Students develop a greater understanding and respect for individual learning differences.

5. **Flexible grouping** and homogeneous grouping by skill level have been demonstrated to be effective for instruction. Changing students within groups is a good practice.

6. **Student engagement time** is a predictor of academic achievement and is defined as the amount of time that students are actively engaged in learning. Students need to be interested in the new concept or skill being taught. If students understand the reasons why learning the new concept is important and how it relates to their lives, they will be engaged. Students should have input in how they would like to be taught, and a teacher needs to create a safe classroom atmosphere that fosters free discussion (e.g., classroom management).

7. **Study skills** are critical to improving student achievement. **Metacognition** is an essential study skill that requires a high degree of self-awareness. Metacognition is thinking and reflecting about learning, what is known, and what is not known. A well-known and time-tested metacognitive technique used to build reading comprehension is SQ3R, which stands for survey, question, read, recite, and review.

## C. Factors in Academic Success or Failure

1. **School climate:** A student's school has high expectations for learning and students believe they can learn. The school provides a safe and positive learning environment. Parents, students, and staff are involved in collaborative decision making. Parents, students, and staff are actively involved in the decisions affecting the school.

2. **Student motivation:** Students who have high intrinsic motivation show increased school engagement and achievement.

3. **Educational practices and policies:** Students do better when schools have formal procedures in place that support evidence-based interventions, early interventions, response to intervention (RTI) process, and *data-based* decision making.

4. **Family involvement:** Families dramatically influence the degree to which children are engaged in school and how they identify themselves as learners.

## D. Student Retention Issues

Grade retention is the practice of keeping a student in the same grade due to academic or maturity concerns. A substantial amount of research *does not* support the use of grade retention. Approximately 15% of American students are held back each year with highest percentages among poor, minority, and inner-city youth.

Research indicates that *achievement declines* within 2 to 3 years postretention. Retained students are more likely to experience significant problems such as interpersonal conflicts with peers, disliking school, behavior problems, and lower self-esteem.

## E. Tracking and Zero-Tolerance Policies

1. **Tracking** is a form of whole-group instruction that is characterized by a set curriculum that is delivered at the same pace for all students within the classroom. Placement into these classes is based solely upon the child's ability level and is, therefore, considered to be an unacceptable approach for the grouping of students. The National Association of School Psychologists (NASP) does *not* generally endorse this practice of tracking.

2. **Zero tolerance** refers to school or district-wide policies that mandate predetermined and typically harsh consequences or punishments for a *wide degree* of rule violation (e.g., drugs, weapons, violence, smoking, and school disruption). Zero-tolerance policies are generally ineffective and are not endorsed. Problems associated with zero-tolerance policies include:

   • Racial disproportionality

   • An increasing incidence of suspensions and expulsions

   • An increase of repeat suspensions

   • Elevated dropout rates

---

**Insider Tip**

Psychologists are not teachers, but they will be called upon to consult with educators about how to teach students with disabilities or other students who are struggling. For the Praxis Exam, understanding learning theories will help you to answer items related to this section. If you remember that all students benefit from individualized instruction tailored toward their specific learning style, some test items will appear straightforward and require common sense. Just like counseling techniques, a multiple and eclectic approach to teaching (multimodal) is considered best practice. Learning by doing and student interest (engagement) are critical teaching aspects.

---

## Summary and Concepts

1. If rewards or punishments are used, they must be given promptly after the behavior. This is called the immediacy principle. Additionally, rewards must be salient (valued by the person) to be effective. Positive reinforcements are more desirable than punishments in learning situations.

2. It is best practice to involve parents and consider the family when a student presents with a learning concern or behavior problem. Always document the time and type of parental contact.

3. NASP endorses parental notification and involvement. Typically, teachers are encouraged to involve parents when a student is having academic or behavioral concerns. On the exam, usually any response option that involves parental contact has a high probability of being the correct answer.

4. Understand the differences between phonological instruction and whole language instruction. Generally, the sounding of letters to form words (phonics) is a very effective instructional method for young readers.

5. NASP endorses the use of positive reinforcement in the classroom. There is a strong movement to support and use a child's strengths as much as possible. This is called a *capacity approach* model.

6. *Token economies* (e.g., point and level systems), although using positive and effective reinforcers, are criticized as not practical because they are cumbersome to implement. Token economies or reward systems are useful if they are easy and practical to maintain.

7. A teaching method that encourages a *task analysis* and breaking a complex task into smaller tasks is a widely accepted practice when teaching new concepts.

8. Teachers should be encouraged to make *learning meaningful* to students by explicitly showing them how a lesson is beneficial to their lives or important to society. Students want to understand "why" they have to learn certain concepts.

9. Many times, effective teachers briefly review with their students the previous day's learning and will explicitly preview the parts of a new assignment before each class. Sometimes the schedule for new learning is written on the board for all to see. (A visual component is important.)

10. Teachers are encouraged to use a *multisensory approach*. It is best practice to use auditory, visual, and tactile methods when teaching. Teachers in middle school and high school sometimes need to be reminded of the many different types of learners. It is interesting that high school lectures appeal mostly to auditory learners.

11. Know the differences between the terms *accommodation* and *modification* as it relates to special education services. Accommodations refer to changes in the environment, such as letting a student use a quiet room to take a test. A modification is actually changing a task so the student can perform. For example, a student who has difficulty with writing might be allowed to complete half the number of questions than her peers.

12. The ultimate goal and role of special education services is to increase students' levels of independence and responsibility.

13. Review curriculum-based assessment (CBA) and curriculum-based measurement (CBM) for the NASP exam. CBA is used in program evaluations, although CBM is commonly used for classroom and instructional intervention planning.

14. According to cognitive-behavioral theorists, learning is supported by mental representations of new concepts merging with existing mental concepts (schema) and through associations (i.e., the pairing of a skill or idea with a reinforcer).

15. Cooperative learning is an effective learning strategy. Review Vygotsky's work. Vygotsky also helped to develop the theory of the Zone of Proximal Development (ZPD).

# 5

# Fifth Test Section: Consultation and Collaboration

School psychologists frequently lend their expertise to students, parents, staff, and other professionals in the community. There are effective methods to employ when involved in consultation or collaboration with other people. At the heart of a successful consultation is to first establish a positive helping relationship. After a rapport is established, the people you are helping will be more receptive to the information you provide them. The most difficult aspect of consultation is to gain trust and not to convey a sense of arrogance as an expert.

There are several theories regarding consultation, but they can be largely divided into direct and indirect approaches. Although direct approaches might be time efficient in the short term, indirect approaches with an emphasis on building another person's skills are methods endorsed by the National Association of School Psychologists (NASP) and may save the psychologist valuable time in the long run.

*Note:* In this chapter, the term "consultant" refers to the school psychologist. The "consultee" is typically a teacher or staff member, and the "client" is the child or student. It should be highlighted that the client can also be a larger system like a school or organization. In organizational consultation, the consultant attempts to make broad structural changes that might be associated with the beliefs and values of the individuals who make up the culture of the organization.

## I. Foundation of Consultation and Collaboration
(*Building Rapport: Factors That Influence Effective Relationships*)

A. **Consultant Personal Characteristics**

1. **Openness, Approachability, and Warmth**: These key traits are built upon one's nonverbal body language, tone of voice, facial expressions, and gestures.

2. **Sincerity and Genuineness**

3. **Trustworthiness and Confidentiality**: The consultee and client believe in your competence and your ability to hold private information. You must have both genuine interest and the skills to help people.

4. **Empathy**: The consultant must have the ability to accurately perceive the feelings and values of the client and communicate this understanding to the client.

5. **Self-Disclosers**: Statements that reveal something personal about oneself are most effective if used sparingly and at the proper time, such as to build rapport or show experience with an issue that might offset challenges.

B. **Student or Client Traits and Factors Influencing Consultation**

1. **Student's Age and Developmental Stage**

2. **Coping Styles:** These may be emotional, reactive, thoughtful, or logical.

   • **Externalizing Coping Styles:** Example of externalized coping involve acting out, behavioral problems, fighting, and disrupting class. Students with this coping style need interventions that are focused on positive skill building.

   • **Internalizing Coping Styles:** Students with internalized styles may develop depression, shut down, or become nonresponsive. The consultant needs to employ strategies that foster rapport and understanding and increases self-confidence and perception of control over situations.

3. **Personality Traits:** These traits represent a student's level of openness, agreeableness, conscientiousness, extroversion, and so on.

## II. Models of Consultation

A. **Consultee-Centered Model**

1. Focus on improving and enhancing competence and skills of the consultee.

2. This *indirectly* helps the client by building skills of consultee.

3. The consultant is considered a problem-solving or skill-building expert.

4. The consultee has knowledge of the problem, issue, or situation at hand but needs skills to properly address the problem.

   • **Role of Consultant**

     ▪ Identify effective treatments for client and teach consultee how to meet client needs. Focus is on the consultee rather than the client and how the consultee deals with the client.

     ▪ Increase knowledge base or skill level of the consultee so the consultee can deal with similar situations in the future.

     ▪ Consultant may have to deal with the consultee's distorted view of the client.

B. **Client-Centered Model**

1. This model is not as favored as the consultee-centered model.

2. The client-centered model focuses on the student.

3. The consultant *directly* helps the client.

4. Interventions provided by the consultant are directed to the child and teaches the student skills.

5. It is effective on a single-case basis but not effective for groups.

6. It is time intensive for the consultant.

## C. Behavioral Model (Applies to Consultee- and Client-Centered Models)

1. The behavioral model is solution focused and collects data to affect behavior change in a person (empirically based model).

2. The goal is to reduce frequency of undesirable behavior by altering the relationship between the student behavior and the environment that prevents consultee from working effectively with the client.

3. This prepares the consultee to deal with similar problems in the future.

   - **Basic Steps of the Behavioral Model**
     - Identify problem (critical stage to target efforts and interventions)
     - Implement plan
     - Monitor effectiveness
     - Evaluate and make needed changes to plan
   - **Conjoint Behavioral Consultation** is a special type of behavioral model that supports meetings with all parties (e.g., parent, student, and staff).

## D. Special Considerations

1. **Multicultural and cross-cultural issues:** A multicultural consultation is a culturally sensitive, indirect service model. The consultant adjusts the consultation services to address the needs and cultural values of the consultee, client, or both. It is critical to respect and value other cultures.

2. **Interagency collaboration and school–community** link the client with community resources or school-based services within the school. Examples of school–community collaboration are:

   - **Child-centered:** Direct service to student such as tutoring or mentoring
   - **Family-centered:** Service to parents or entire families such as parenting workshops, family counseling, and family assistance
   - **School-centered:** Donation of money or equipment, staff development, or classroom assistance
   - **Community-centered:** Outreach programs, artwork and science exhibits, and after-school programs

3. **Consultation With Interpreters:** The use of interpreters is encouraged and necessary to build rapport with families and students who do not speak English. When using interpreters, be mindful of speech rate and use brief, simple statements so the interpreter can relay the information efficiently.

4. **Barriers to Collaboration and Consultation**

   - Consultee or client resists participation
   - Client is unable to make a time commitment
   - Funding problems for community collaboration
   - Lack of leadership
   - Communication difficulties
   - Unclear goals or unfocused goals
   - Adversarial relationships with community experts (e.g., medical doctors)

---

**Insider Tip**

Although there are many consultation models geared toward specific people, it is important to focus on the benefits and liabilities of the consultee-centered model. An essential idea to keep in mind is that NASP seems to endorse the indirect service model, which seeks to build the consultee's skills (i.e., teacher's skills) so the consultee can help the student. If you have questions on the NASP exam regarding the most effective model, it is probably the indirect service model. Read Dr. Gerald Caplan's work on consultation models.

## Summary and Concepts

1. The client-centered consultation benefits only one client (i.e., the student). For example, when a teacher has a problem with a student, the school psychologist intervenes with the student. This method can produce desired results, but it is time consuming. Generally speaking, it is best practice to teach staff how to help themselves.

2. The consultee-centered consultation benefits the teacher by building skills that might be used to help numerous other people. In other words, the psychologist helps the teacher develop new skills to support the students. This model seems to be best practice at the present time.

3. Know the primary benefits and liabilities of the previous two models. Be able to compare and contrast models of consultation.

4. The program-centered administrative consultation model benefits an entire program or school. For example, a school psychologist performs an in-service for a school.

5. In a consultee-centered administrative model a school psychologist teaches skills to other key administrators to effect change at many schools or a district.

6. A common problem-solving consultation format involves the following steps:

   a. Define the problem; be specific

   b. Analyze the problem and collect data if necessary

   c. Plan an intervention-monitor and modify as necessary

   d. Evaluate your outcomes, compare pre–post data, and make changes

7. Other consultation models: The ecological (systems) model examines how a person's behavior is being maintained within various settings and systems. The process consultation model uses workgroups, feedback, and coordination among groups.

8. Study the special considerations related to particular consultation cases. Some considerations include cultural issues, barriers to clear communication, barriers to effective consultation, difficulties with community experts (e.g., medical doctors), and family consultation factors.

# 6

# Sixth Test Section: Ethical, Legal, and Professional Foundations

Regardless of the professional area, ethical problems are some of the most challenging questions to answer. Do not underestimate the complexity of the ethical and legal issues school psychologists face. It will be well worth your time to have a firm grasp of National Association of School Psychologists (NASP) guidelines that govern the ethical behavior of school psychologists. Many ethical questions on the Praxis™ Exam will not have a clear answer but rather degrees of correctness. Most ethical response options will have components that are correct, but look for small details that spoil the answer. In other words, ethical questions are best answered by a process of elimination; consider why an answer could *not* be correct versus why it must be right. It might be helpful if you understand NASP's general positions on all the services provided by practitioners. The following are examples of typical ethical issues faced by psychologists:

- School psychologists should always seek professional consultation when unsure about administering a new cognitive test.
- Psychologists must not practice outside of their area of expertise.
- Practitioners must secure informed consent from parents when providing services to children.

Although ethical and legal questions garner the majority of attention in this section, do not forget this area also includes professional foundations. Professional foundations include important historical aspects and technical terms related to school psychology. Due to the broad nature of history, focus your efforts on key *landmark* historical events, not trivia or specific dates.

## I. Major Ethical Guidelines and Standards for Practice

### A. NASP Ethical Principles

*Note:* On the Praxis Exam, all ethical questions should be answered based on the following principles. It is worth memorizing the following four principles. For any given test question, determine whether each response option violates any part of the following principles. If an option violates even one of the principles, it is not the correct answer.

1. **Respect the dignity and rights of all persons:** Practitioners demonstrate respect for the autonomy of persons and their right to self-determination, respect for privacy, and a commitment to just and fair treatment of all persons.

2. **Professional competence and responsibility:** School psychologists must practice within the boundaries of their competence and use scientific knowledge from psychology and education to benefit people. They should accept responsibility for the choices they make.

3. **Honesty and integrity in relationships:** Psychologists must be truthful and adhere to their professional standards. Practitioners must be honest about their qualifications, competencies, and roles. They work in cooperation with other professional disciplines to help students and families. Avoid multiple relationships that diminish their professional effectiveness.

4. **Responsibility to schools, families, communities, the profession, and society:** School psychologists promote positive school, family, and community environments. Psychologists must respect the law and encourage strict ethical conduct. One can advance one's professional excellence by mentoring less experienced practitioners and contribute to the school psychology knowledge base.

B. **Additional and Specific Guidelines**

1. **Test use and misuse:** Practitioners must comprehend the technical aspects of psychometrics, testing, and measurement of human traits. Use multiple sources of information when evaluating students. Maintain record and test confidentiality and security.

2. **Confidentiality:** Practitioners must adhere to strict confidentiality principles. For example, obtain written consent before sharing information, destroy documents before throwing them away, do not discuss confidential information, and make sure people know the limits of confidentiality (e.g., safety and harm issues).

3. **Supervision standards:** Practitioners should know key aspects of proper supervision. Important aspects include providing at least 2 hours of supervision per week, holding proper license and credentials, and maintaining 1 supervisor for 10 interns.

4. **Private practice standards:** Guidelines under this area involve financial issues. For example, do not charge people for services that are provided by the school district that employs you. Do not accept money for referrals. Do not engage in private-practice work during school hours. Provide honest and complete information about yourself and your services when advertising your practice.

5. **Reporting of abuse and safety:** Know abuse laws and your mandated duties. A psychologist's duty to protect children is his or her highest responsibility. The duty to protect children outweighs confidentiality. Safety issues

are critical, and you have a duty to warn others of harm. (This is a likely Praxis Exam item.)

6. **Child benefit is always the focus:** Psychologists should consult with teachers and staff, but do not counsel adults; focus efforts on the child. Provide information and resources to adults in need, but provide intervention to children.

7. **Provide balanced information:** Give research information on medications to parents, but do not pressure parents about medication. Provide balanced opinions about the benefits and liabilities of treatments or approaches to student issues.

C. **Grievances**

**Complaints about an NASP member**: The following are guidelines to understand when engaged in an ethical dispute:

1. Complaints must be made by an identified person (not anonymous).

2. It is important to try to resolve concerns with the individual before filing a complaint. People who file a complaint do not have to be NASP members.

3. An ethics committee will decide whether to hear the case.

4. An ethics committee will examine the evidence and determine if the complaint has merit and whether the complaint is in violation of NASP ethics.

5. Notification in writing will be granted to an individual who has been filed against.

6. An ethics committee will attempt to resolve conflicts through discussion and participation of all parties in the dispute.

7. Possible actions by ethics committee:
   - Dismiss complaint
   - Seek more information
   - Corrective measures
   - Member placed on probation
   - Require member to give compensation or provide an apology
   - Require additional training and skill development
   - Expulsion from NASP

*Note:* **Additional Internet Resource:** NASP Ethical Conduct and Professional Practices www.nasponline.org/standards/ethics/ethical-conduct-professional-practices.aspx

## II. Legal Considerations

A. **Student Issues**

1. **Aversive Procedures:** These are discouraged and should be considered a last resort for students (e.g., self-injurious behaviors may need temporary restraining). Informed parental consent is necessary.

2. **Corporal Punishment:** NASP strongly opposes the use of corporal punishment in schools. Psychologists should educate others about the harm that corporal punishment causes children.

3. **Courts (Position):** Courts have ruled that schools should apply discipline in a fair, nondiscriminatory manner, school rules should be clearly stated, and the consequences for breaking rules understood by all students.

4. **Suspension and Expulsion:** Schools have the authority to suspend students. Short-term suspensions are 10 days or less. *Special education students must have a special review meeting* if they are suspended 10 days. The Individuals with Disabilities Education Act (**IDEA**) contains *special protections for students with disabilities.* Students with disabilities who violate a school rule may be removed from school for no more than 10 cumulative days. For suspensions less than 10 days, schools are not required to provide educational services.

5. **Change of Placement Because of Disciplinary Removals:** A change of placement occurs if:
   - The removal is **more than 10 consecutive** days.
   - The behavior is substantially similar in all instances that lead to the removal.
   - There have been additional factors such as the length of each removal, the total number of times the student has been removed, or the proximity of the removals to each other.
   - **A school psychologist must also provide a functional behavioral assessment (FBA)** to determine the cause of the behavior.

6. **Manifestation Determination:** A manifestation meeting is conducted by the individualized education program (IEP) team to determine whether or not the student's behavior warrants a 10-day suspension or if the expulsion was a result of a disability. This meeting must be held within 10 days of the change of placement decision. If the behavior was a manifestation of the student's disability, the team must provide an FBA and implement a behavior plan for the student. The child may return to the original school placement or be placed in another school if it is part of the new FBA plan and agreed upon by the team.

   *Note:* If the behavior was not determined to be a manifestation of the child's disability, disciplinary procedures may be applied to the child in the same manner as children without disabilities, except the child still receives the same additional protections under IDEA such as free and appropriate public education (FAPE).

7. **Special Suspension and Expulsion Considerations:** Schools may place a child with a disability in an interim placement for 45 days, regardless of manifestation determination, if the student carried a weapon to school; inflicted serious bodily harm on another individual; or knowingly sold, used, or possessed drugs.
   - Parents or schools can appeal the manifestation determination to a hearing officer.
   - A child who has a disability but has not yet received an IEP can have the same protections under IDEA if the school or parents suspect that the student has a disability.

8. **Least Restrictive Environment (LRE):** An LRE is mandated for children with disabilities. The section of IDEA that pertains to LRE reads as follows:

> To the maximum extent appropriate, children with disabilities should be educated with children who are not disabled, and special classes, separate schooling, or other removal of children with disabilities from the regular educational environment should occur only when the nature or severity of the disability is such that education in regular classes with the use of supplementary aids and services cannot be achieved satisfactorily.

B. **Legal Considerations for Practitioners**

1. **Malpractice:** Lawsuits typically occur if there is harm to a student as a result of the professional interaction. The likelihood of a practitioner being sued is less than 1%.

2. **Supervision:** Even though interns are supervised, both supervisor and intern can be sued.

3. **Negligence:** Of all legal suits, negligence is the most common offense and mostly occurs when there is student suicide or injury that could have been reasonably prevented by the practitioner.

## III. Specific Laws Relevant to School Psychology

- **Education for All Handicapped Children Act (EAHCA), 1975**
  - The first special education law in the United States
  - Often referred to as P.L. 94-142
  - After various amendments, the **name was changed to IDEA** (Individuals with Disabilities Education Act)

- **IDEA, 2004**
  - Applies to students with the following disabilities: autism; deaf-blindness; deafness; hearing impairment; mental retardation; multiple disabilities; orthopedic impairments or other health impairments; emotional disturbance; specific learning disability; speech or language impairment; traumatic brain injury (TBI); visual impairment, including blindness.
  - Mandates FAPE for all children with disabilities.
  - Mandates that students receiving special education services are placed in an LRE.
  - States **must not require the use of the discrepancy model** and must **permit the use of a response to intervention (RTI) model**. IDEA may permit the use of other research-based procedures for identifying learning disabilities (LD). **(This point is a key concept of IDEA and may be asked on the Praxis Exam.)** Note that NASP endorses the use of RTI, but schools can actually still use other models such as the discrepancy model to determine eligibility for services.

- **No Child Left Behind (NCLB), 2001**
  - Purpose is to close the achievement gap
  - Targets high-risk schools

- Mandates statewide formal assessments for grades 3 to 8. Each state must strive for academic proficiency for students or face possible consequences by governing agencies.
- Made public school choice available for students at schools that are low performing for 2 years.
- Act requires highly qualified teachers for public schools.

- **Individuals with Disabilities Education Improvement Act (IDEIA), 2004**
  - Students must be assessed with nondiscriminatory assessments and decisions must be made by a multidisciplinary team that includes parents.
  - RTI can be used.
  - Elaborates and further defines parental safeguards and rights presented in IDEA.
  - Provides funds for children from birth to age 3.

- **Family Educational Rights and Privacy Act (FERPA), 1974**
  - Schools must adhere to strict student record-keeping procedures.
  - FERPA recordkeeping laws are designed to protect confidentiality and allow parents access to educational records.

- **The Rehabilitation Act: Section 504, 1973**
  - This is not a special education law but is part of the Americans with Disabilities Act (ADA).
  - Provides a broader definition of "handicap" than "disability" under IDEA (Sped Law).
  - Section 504 prohibits discrimination against otherwise qualifying individuals on the basis of a handicapping condition in any program receiving federal funds.

- **Zero Reject Principle**
  - Established Child Find, which requires states to locate and identify children with disabilities and provide them with full educational opportunity, regardless of the severity of the disability.

**Special Education Procedural Safeguards**: Know key procedural safeguards and the timeframes for compliance as required by law.

- **Complaints**: Must be filed within *2 years of problem or dispute.*
- **Resolution meetings**: Within *15 days* of receiving the complaint, schools must convene a meeting.
- **Due process hearings**: Parents have the right to request a third-party hearing officer for special education disputes.
- **Consent**: Written parental consent *must be obtained before an evaluation.* Schools may proceed without consent for triennial reviews if documented reasonable efforts have been made to contact parent(s).
- **Notice**: Prior written notice must be given to parents for the initiation or change of a student's identification, evaluation, placement, change of service,

or educational programming. Remember, there is a difference between a notice and consent.

- **Procedural safeguards notice:** A parents' rights booklet must be provided to parents *once per year* and at the initial evaluation if a parent requests it and if a complaint has been filed. This may be posted on the school's website.

- **IEP meetings:** Must be held within *60 days* after a parent signs consent for initial evaluation and *once a year* after that. Re-evaluations are held *every 3 years*.

- **Special education team:** The team must consist of parents, at least one regular education teacher, at least one of the child's special education teachers, a representative of the school who is qualified to provide or supervise the provision of services, someone who can interpret the evaluation results. It may also consist of other individuals who have knowledge or special expertise about the child as well as the child when appropriate.

- **Excusal from meeting**: A parent needs to submit a written note to the school that gives permission for a member of the IEP team to be excused from the meeting. However, someone must be present who can explain assessment results.

## IV. Foundations and Pioneers of School Psychology

### Timeline of Important Developments

*Note:* It is unlikely you will have to memorize specific dates. However, it might be beneficial if you know the timeframe for the origin of psychology, when school psychology was accepted by professional association, and important legislative acts that impacted the field (e.g., PL-94–142; 1975). A primary resource for historical events can be found in Fagan and Wise (2007).

The following timeline is based on Fagan and Wise's work.

- **1870–1909  Origins of psychology as a professional field**
  - Emergence of empirically valid psychological tests
  - Psychology gains form as a profession
  - Initial psychological practices emerge
- **1910–1929  Expansion and acceptance of psychology as a professional discipline**
- **1930–1939  First major regulations and laws for practice**
- **1940–1949  Accreditation bodies form**
- **1950–1959  School psychology subfield forms**
- **1960–1969  Professional growth and training programs develop, NASP founded**
- **1970–1979  Strict modern regulations and laws appear, association's expansion, first special education laws**
- **1980–1989  NASP evolution, first NASP exam**

- **1990–1999** **Growth and reforms, new identity considered**
- **2000–present** **Expansion of NASP identity and practice**
- **2001** **Passage of NCLB**
- **2004** **Reauthorization of IDEA**
- **2008** **NASP celebrates fortieth anniversary**
- **2010** **NASP adopts new professional standards**

### Internet and Resources for Standards and Practices

- 2010 NASP Professional Standards: http://www.nasponline.org/standards/2010standards.aspx
- NASP Principles for Professional Ethics 2010: www.nasponline.org/standards/2010standards/1_%20Ethical%20Principles.pdf

### Supplemental Concepts, Considerations, and Key Experts

- **William Wundt** is considered the **founding father of psychology** (experimental, structuralism) and started the first psychology lab in Germany in the **1870s**. He wrote the first widely regarded psychology paper on the physiology of psychology.
- The **father of *school* psychology** is **Lightner Witmer**. Dr. Witmer established a clinic at the University of Pennsylvania in 1896. He combined educational and psychological services to help students with learning and behavioral problems.
- The **first *school* psychologist** was **Arnold Gessell.** Gessell became the first school psychologist in **1915**. He believed that development in children was a parallel and orderly process. Gessell is believed to have been the first to develop tests that measured development in children.
- **B. F. Skinner** (1904–1990) was a major contributor to the field of behaviorism. Skinner believed that all behavior was shaped and maintained by consequences that followed behavior. His theories are also steeped in empirical methods. Skinnerian principles are primarily used today in school systems due to their practical and effective applications.
- **Albert Bandura** believed that cognition helped to drive behavior. Bandura added balance to the strict beliefs of the behavioristic theories of Skinner.
- Much of the work school psychologists conduct is based on the critical premise that key human traits fall on a **normal curve** that forms the shape of a bell **(bell curve).** Several experts were involved in the initial observance of the bell curve in the 1700s, but reference **Francis Galton** for his work on the theory in 1880. **Alfred Binet** was one of the first scientists to measure the construct of intelligence and its relation to the normal curve.
- One of the most comprehensive but easy to understand resources about testing, measurement, and psychometrics is the **Web Center for Social Research Methods**: www.socialresearchmethods.net
- Factor analysis and two-factor analysis, which are key statistical methods, provide validation for the theory of intelligence tests that are based on "g."

"g" correlates with other factors to varying degrees to create human thinking ability. **Spearman and Thurstone** both contributed substantially to psychometrics and cognitive testing. Spearman, especially, helped develop factor analysis.

- **Lewis Terman** studied gifted children and believed in cognitive ability testing. He also believed that bright children should have resources allocated to their special needs. Terman helped to revise the Stanford-Binet cognitive test for use with American children. In America, Terman's revised Standford-Binet intelligence test was the first to be employed in 1916.

- The current theory on intelligence is that intelligence is based on a complex interplay of genetics (heredity) and environmental factors. Intelligence is closely associated with an ability to adapt to one's environment and apply information. A key expert to suggest this balanced view of intelligence was **Dr. Philip Vernon**. In contrast to Vernon, **Arthur Jensen** is a prominent researcher known for his work in behavioral genetics. Jensen believes that intelligence has a strong genetic basis.

- Several widely adopted cognitive ability tests that are currently used by school psychologists are based on the **Cattell–Horn** theory of crystallized and fluid intelligence. Fluid intelligence is associated with reasoning with novel problems, whereas crystallized intelligence is related to acquired knowledge and skills. Know that the most recent theoretical basis for cognitive tests, such as the WISC-IV and DAS-II, is the **Cattell–Horn–Carroll** or **CHC theory** and is *statistically* derived. CHC adds additional narrow abilities to the crystallized and fluid view of intelligence.

---

### Insider Tip

The Ethical, Legal, and Professional Foundations domain of the Praxis Exam seems to have more items to memorize than other parts of the exam. Although it is unlikely you will have specific dates to remember, you probably will have to know the names of landmark laws and legal cases, which are listed in the following Summary and Concepts section. You might have one or two questions regarding pioneering or venerable experts in the field, but it is probably not a good idea to memorize all experts in the field. Study only the well-known names and significant contributors to the field of psychology. Finally, it is critical to know what constitutes poor practices and what psychological practices are illegal. As mentioned in the Introduction, key ethical guidelines involve informed consent and practices that benefit children while safeguarding their dignity.

---

## Summary and Concepts

1. NASP endorses the practice of securing parental notification and supports parental and community involvement. As a consequence of NASP's endorsements, answer relevant test questions that have a positive parental or community involvement choice.

2. Study **IDEA Public Law 94–142** very thoroughly. Note the changes in the IDEA in a more recent act called the IDEIA. The IDEA act gives the right to a free and appropriate public education in the LRE for all students.

3. **FERPA** was passed in 1974 and is sometimes called the Buckley Amendment. This act gives families the right to review the records of their children and the files must be kept confidential. The public and other people who do not have legal privileges cannot review a student's file. Confidentiality is central to this law.

4. **Section 504** is a civil rights law and guarantees access to a school building and to a school's curriculum. Many people mistakenly believe this is an educational law, but it is important to remember the Office of Civil Rights, not the Department of Education, enforces it. Section 504 is a law governing the rights of handicapped people. Students with hearing or vision problems sometimes fall under this law. Also, in some cases, children with attention deficit hyperactivity disorder (ADHD) are said to have a physical handicap and, therefore, are entitled to have full access to the general curriculum.

5. ***Brown v. Board of Education*** states that educational facilities are not allowed to segregate according to race.

6. ***Hobson v. Hansen*** ruled that schools must provide equal educational opportunities despite a family's socioeconomic status (SES). Review laws dealing with ability tracking.

7. ***Diana v. State Board of Education*** states that assessments must be administered in the native language of the student in order to validate minority testing practices. This is similar to another case, *Guadalupe v. Temple School District*. In this case, it was ruled that students cannot be identified as mentally retarded unless they were properly assessed by considering the student's primary language and had scores at least 2 standard deviations below the mean.

8. ***Larry P. v. Riles*** was a landmark case in California that ruled that the percentage of minority students placed in special education classrooms couldn't exceed the percentage in the representative population. This ruling was based on the fact that there was an overrepresentation of minorities classified as mentally retarded.

9. ***PASE v. Hannon*** is a pro-special education ruling that endorsed the use of standardized tests as long as they are not culturally biased and are used with several other measures.

10. ***Marshall v. Georgia*** is also a pro-special education ruling that stood in contrast to the *Larry P.* case. The Marshall ruling stated that the percentage of minorities placed in special education can exceed the percentage in the representative population as long as the appropriate and proper steps for placement were followed.

11. ***Honig v. Doe*** states that special education students must have a manifestation hearing to review placement if they are suspended for more than 10 days.

12. Gifted education, at this point in time, is not federally funded. Federal law does not require services or funding for those students who are gifted

(IQ > 130). However, the reader should research this area of law to ascertain whether laws are different in individual states.

13. ***Rowley v. Board of Education*** is an important landmark case wherein the judge stated public schools *do not have to provide the best education, but rather an adequate education*. In other words, schools do not have to provide a Cadillac; a Ford is acceptable. (Hint: Never repeat the previous statement to a parent.)

14. The ***Tarasoff*** case is a well-known case that is an interesting story. In short, the court ruled that a school district has a **duty to warn** the parents if their child is in danger. (This is important for anti-bullying programs.)

15. ***Lau v. Nichols*** ruled that schools must provide accommodations for ESL students.

16. **Child Find Law** for children 0 to 3 years old was based on PL-94-457, Education of the Handicapped Act. PL-94-457 authorized early intervention for toddlers and families.

17. The **Perkins Act** gives rights to transition special educational students into vocational programs. Provides occupational access.

18. Be familiar with **NCLB** and how it impacts school districts. A notable feature of this law is that it requires schools to employ "highly" qualified staff. Schools must meet high standards that are gauged by objective measures (e.g., standardized tests). Schools that do not meet NCLB standards are at risk for losing federal money and support.

19. ***Tatro v. Irving Independent School District*** was a Supreme Court case that ruled that schools must provide medical services that do not require a medical doctor to be perform them to students who require such services, even if the child needs full-time attention from a nurse.

# 7

# Special Content Areas: Neuropsychology, Traumatic Brain Injury, and Other Concepts

This chapter contains content that does not fit neatly under the other major areas noted earlier. In the first edition of this book, it was mentioned that neuropsychology would have an impact on the field of school psychology. Since that time, neuropsychology has greatly influenced school psychology and has even created a new subfield called school neuropsychology. Recent graduates in school psychology might have a knowledge advantage over veteran school psychologists because neuropsychological course work is now required by many graduate programs. Neuropsychological research is especially dynamic, and advances within this field are occurring frequently.

In my opinion, the largest areas of influence that neuropsychology has on school psychology is within the area of pediatric brain injury. In the future, several school psychologists will serve on or lead brain injury resource teams (BIRT) and help manage concussions at the school level. Brain injury issues are readily applicable to the practice of school psychology as practitioners routinely measure and assess brain-based functions typically associated with brain dysfunction. In fact, in more than any other profession, psychologists are the experts in the measurement of brain functioning.

Do not expect many questions on the National Association of School Psychologists (NASP) exam regarding the following areas. You might only have two or three questions. However, future NASP tests will likely have more questions related to these topics because of their recognized importance.

## Neuropsychology

Neuropsychology is the study of **brain–behavior relationships**. School-neuropsychology is the study of brain–behavior relationships as they apply in a school setting and how neurological factors might impact a student's academic functioning. School neuropsychologists believe that all learning dysfunctions, behavioral disorders, and emotional disorders are brain-based issues. By understanding the neurological underpinnings of brain functioning, school neuropsychologists are better able to provide answers to parents about why their child is having difficulty in school.

## I. Basic Neuroanatomy

At the most basic brain level are primary cells called neurons. Billions of neurons are connected to each other throughout the entire brain to create a neurological network. The network of neurons is connected to tightly bundled, specialized neurons called nuclei. These neuronal bundles are found in localized areas of the brain that perform particular functions (Carter, 2009; Sweeney, 2009). These specific brain regions and their primary functions are illustrated in Figure 7.1. For a virtual and interactive tour of the brain reference, visit www.pbs.org/wnet/brain/3d.

Scientists have various ways to organize the brain and its functions. One way to conceptualize brain processes is to organize its function starting from how the brain develops physiologically. The first areas of the brain to develop are the regions located at the base of the brain. Basal brain areas are generally related to basic physiological functions. For example, two important basal sections are the brain stem and cerebellum. The brain stem and cerebellum control involuntary functions such as breathing, heart rate, gross-motor movement, and arousal. Brain injuries to these basal areas are extremely serious as such injuries can be fatal (e.g., can stop heartbeat, breathing, and consciousness).

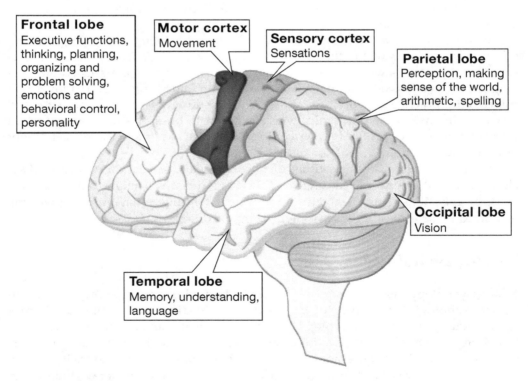

**FIGURE 7.1**   Specific functions of brain areas (Pubweb, 2011).

The upper regions of the brain are associated with complex functions commonly associated with sensory processes, information processing, and behavior. These highly evolved brain areas influence verbal communication, fine motor movement, vision, emotions, rational thought, comprehension, and reasoning.

### A. Functional Areas (Lobes)

There are four major lobes of the brain that play a major role in processing, information, thinking, memory, and regulating behavior.

1. **Frontal Lobe:** This lobe is responsible for **executive functions**. This area does not necessarily process information as much as it controls other aspects of the brain (e.g., it is the brain manager or executive). This lobe helps in planning future actions and regulating behavior. It is also responsible for cognitive flexibility and helps people shift to different aspects of problem solving or topics.

2. **Parietal Lobe:** Located roughly on the top portion of the brain, this area helps to assimilate body sensations (i.e., somatosensory). Sensory disorders are typically associated with the parietal lobe. As a secondary role, this lobe also helps with developing symbolic associations and math skills and with integrating information.

3. **Temporal Lobe:** Located on the right and left side of the brain, this lobe of the brain primarily processes auditory information and language. The temporal lobe is implicated in **reading problems** and phonological processing difficulties.

4. **Occipital Lobe:** Located at the back of the head. This area is responsible for processing visual information.

### B. Hemisphere Operations

In addition to specific brain lobe functions, another broad conceptualization of brain function has been observed by researchers for decades. It is a commonly held—but simplified—belief that the **right hemisphere** of the brain is associated with creativity, holistic thinking, novel information processing, and visual–spatial processes. In contrast to the right, the **left hemisphere** of the brain is concerned with language, verbal information, sequences, and factual (learned or familiar) information (see Figure 7.2).

Currently, a refinement of the right versus left model involves an emphasis on new versus routine information processing. Some experts believe the right half of the brain is responsible for processing novel information. Once the novel information is processed and understood, it is transferred to the left side of the brain where it becomes part of the person's knowledge base. The left side stores routine, familiar, and factual information. This previously learned information is later retrieved and used when a person engages in routines or responds to the environment (Fiorello & Hale, 2004).

### C. Key Neurological Concepts

1. Although there are areas of the brain (lobes) that are primarily responsible for specific functions, the brain works as a whole unit and needs all parts working together in order to function properly.

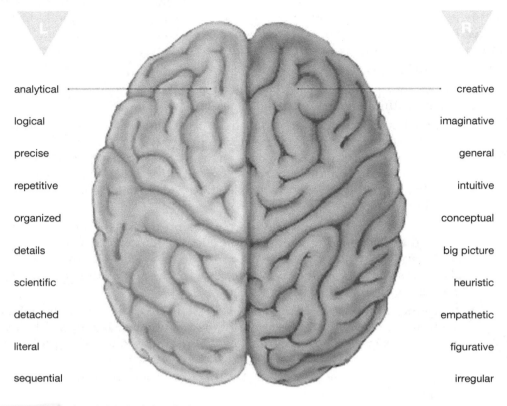

analytical · · · · · · · · · · · · · · · · · · · · · · · · · · · · · · · · · · · creative

logical                                                              imaginative

precise                                                                  general

repetitive                                                               intuitive

organized                                                             conceptual

details                                                                big picture

scientific                                                             heuristic

detached                                                              empathetic

literal                                                                 figurative

sequential                                                              irregular

**FIGURE 7.2**   Left and right brain hemispheres (BIAA, 2011).

2. It appears that no one particular area is responsible for storing all **memories,** but, rather, memories are stored and diffused throughout the brain. A major part of the brain called the **hippocampus** is implicated in *forming* memories because of its role in associating emotions with events.

3. The **amygdala** is associated with **emotions** and emotional responses.

4. The corpus callosum is a bundle of nerves that connects both halves of the brain and allows for communication between the two hemispheres.

5. Attention deficit hyperactivity disorder (ADHD) is associated with a dysfunction and neurochemical issue within the frontal lobes. However, ADHD research is still emerging.

6. The cerebral cortex is associated with higher order reasoning.

7. Broca's area and Wernicke's area are implicated in speech and language problems and reading difficulties. Broca's area is linked to expressive language, whereas Wernicke's area is associated with receptive language.

8. Aphasia is the inability to use language, and agnosia is the inability to identify seen objects.

9. The limbic system (part of the lower brain) houses those areas responsible for our emotions (e.g., amygdala, hippocampus, and others).

10. Neurochemicals (brain chemicals):
    - **Dopamine**: This neurochemical is involved in producing positive moods and emotions. Dopamine is associated with reward, pleasure, and novelty seeking. It is implicated in Parkinson's disease and ADHD.
    - **Endorphin**: Endorphins are a natural opiate similar to morphine that are released to moderate pain.
    - **Serotonin** helps regulate relaxation, sleep, and mood. An imbalance in serotonin is implicated in clinical depression.

## II. Traumatic Brain Injury

A recent legal development is that federal law allows for traumatic brain injury (TBI) to be its own diagnostic category on individualized education programs (IEPs). Like learning disabilities, a brain injury must impair the functioning of a student to a marked degree and have an educational impact to qualify for special education services. Students who have a TBI typically also have a medical diagnosis of a moderate or severe brain injury. Mild brain injuries, like concussions, generally do not qualify children for IEP services due to their temporary nature.

There is neither a solitary test for a brain injury nor a typical profile for brain injury. Each brain injury manifests itself differently in individuals. With the previous statements in mind, common neurological functions that are sensitive to brain insults are processing speed, attention, and memory. Post brain injury, crystallized skills and knowledge generally returns, whereas fluid abilities are prone to disruption.

The following are brief concepts and information that might be useful to remember about children and brain injuries.

A. **Key TBI Concepts**

1. An excellent resource for brain injury in children is the Brain Injury Association of America (www.biausa.org).

2. Traumatic brain injury is sometimes referred to as acquired brain injury. TBI causes over 50,000 deaths a year and is a leading cause of death in children under 18 years old.

3. Research in the area of head injury is advancing at a very fast pace and some new theories are contradicting theories from just a few years ago. For example, it was previously believed it was better to have a brain injury as a child because a child's brain could heal itself more effectively than an adult's. Current thinking has significantly changed and now it is believed that a child's brain is more vulnerable to damage than an adult's.

4. Even mild concussions (e.g., mild brain injury and mild traumatic brain injury [mTBI]) can cause persistent difficulties. If concussion symptoms do not resolve in several weeks, then the student may have postconcussion syndrome (PCS). Children may seem okay after a hit to the head, but damage and swelling may occur.

5. Children with significant TBI require frequent assessments because they may show drastic changes in the first year of recovery. Both cognitive and personality changes could be evident after a TBI.

6. There is debate over neuro-elasticity (plasticity), or how the brain heals itself. Current research illustrates that children are more at risk for permanent brain damage than adults. The younger the developmental age, the more at risk the person is for various types of long-term problems. Age at the incident of TBI and type of TBI are important for assessment and planning interventions.

7. Cognitive tests can help determine the functioning of the brain (i.e., what the person can do) after a head trauma. Cognitive tests for older TBI victims typically show a large amount of variation between subtest scores. However, very young children sometimes show uniformly low subtest scores. Processing speed, fluid abilities, and behavioral and emotional changes are typically noted post injury. However, there is no classic profile of TBI.

8. Symptoms and signs of TBI include headaches, sleep disruptions, mood swings, personality changes, light or noise sensitivity, and balance problems.

9. Interventions for TBI victims should focus on what the child can do and build upon those strengths (i.e., capacity or strength-based approach). Half-day schedules have been effective in teaching students with TBI as cognitive fatigue is a primary trait of students with brain injuries.

10. In moderate to severe TBI cases, errorless learning techniques have proved effective. Visual charts, repetition of new information, and repetition of skills are also key strategies to employ with students who have TBI.

# Other Important Concepts Relevant to School Psychology

## *Models of Basic Information Processing (Cognitive Psychology)*

### I. Basic (Simplistic) Information Processing Model
Information (Input) ———— Central Processing ———— Expressive (Output)

### II. Complex Model

```
┌─────────────────────────┐
│   Selective Attention   │
│ (Person pays attention  │
│    to a stimulus.)      │
└─────────────────────────┘
            │
            ▼
┌─────────────────────────┐      ┌──────────────────────────────┐
│ "Encoding" information  │─────▶│ Information is rehearsed and  │
│  into short-term        │      │ associated with prior        │
│  memory.                │      │ knowledge. If not, then      │
│  (Input)                │      │ information is forgotten and │
└─────────────────────────┘      │ not stored.                  │
                                 └──────────────────────────────┘
┌─────────────────────────┐◀────────────┘
│ Information is "coded"   │
│ and stored into         │
│ long-term memory.       │
│ (Storage)               │
└─────────────────────────┘
            │
            ▼
┌─────────────────────────┐
│ Information is retrieved │
│ or "decoded" from       │
│ memory. Expression.     │
│ (Output)                │
└─────────────────────────┘
```

- *Note:* A breakdown or problem can occur at any level of the information-processing model. For example, people may have difficulty learning because they have not properly "encoded" the information. On the other hand, people may have properly encoded the information and understand concepts but cannot retrieve (decode) the details of the information.

- The average person can hold approximately **seven to eight bits of information in short-term memory**. Short-term memory should not be confused with working memory. In working memory, one must perform an activity while holding ideas, thoughts, and information *online*.

- People tend to remember the first and last aspects of new information they see or hear. This is called the **primacy memory effect** (referring to the first piece of information) and *recency* **effect** (referring to the last piece of information).

# Appendix

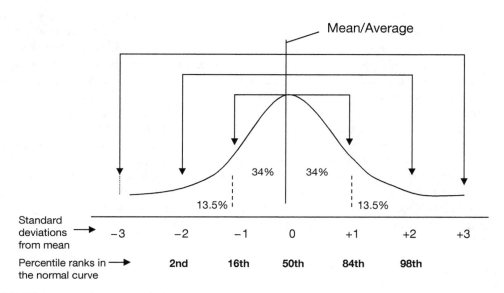

**FIGURE A.1**   The normal distribution of human traits or bell curve.

Approximately 68% of all people fall within 1 standard deviation of the mean (34% + 34% = 68%).
Percentiles (listed on the bottom of the figure) are not percentages and are not equal interval measurements like standard scores.

# Note to the Reader

The following practice exams contain questions that are similar in both style and content to the actual items found on the Praxis™ Exam. However, it is important to note that there are several versions of this test offered by the Educational Testing Service (ETS). Consequently, test questions and exam formats periodically change. For example, some students may be administered a test that contains a few questions with four response options, while some test takers may receive a version that includes test items with more response choices. Because the primary mission of this guide is to help the student study effectively, but also in a time-efficient manner, these practice tests are designed with four response options instead of five or six. Having four response options does not significantly alter the difficulty of the sample test (25% vs. 20% correct guess rate), but it does allow the reader more time to study complex test questions, which is the main point of taking practice tests. Questions that the reader answered incorrectly should be flagged as evidence of content that needs further review and study.

# Practice Tests

The following practice exams do not contain the exact questions that are found in the real Praxis™ Exam. However, several items, fundamental concepts, and the format are very similar to the actual exam. It is important to remember that most exam questions involve constructs that have myriad ancillary facts associated with them. Therefore, the reader needs to fully understand all the related concepts each question addresses.

During this trial run, ask yourself several questions about the underlying concept for each item. You may even ask yourself how each test question could be asked differently. It is strongly recommended that you make notes regarding the questions you need to know more about. Notice the types of questions you miss the most. Are the missed questions the legal and ethical ones or the assessment ones? Also, be familiar with keywords and how those keywords are usually found in the correct response choice.

The benefit of taking practice tests is that it is an excellent way to study for the real test. Practice testing hones skills such as time management and response selection. It also decreases your anxiety because it takes some of the mystery out of the real exam.

Ready yourself as you would in an *actual testing situation*. Treat the following practice tests as real tests. Turn the page, read the directions carefully, and begin!

# Practice Test I

**DIRECTIONS: You have 2 hours to complete the following test. Be mindful to keep strict time limits. Although two answer choices might be true, select the one that is better. Do not leave any questions blank. If you change your answer, erase your previous choice thoroughly.** (Advice: Put a small check by those questions that are very difficult to answer and move on to the next item. Remember to go back to the marked questions and complete them after going through all the questions and before finishing the test.) **Answers are provided following these tests.**

**Ready?**                                    **Start Timing: 120 minutes**

1. Sue is a second grade student who struggles with reading. It happens that Sue's teacher lives next door to a reading specialist in the school district. Sue's teacher asked her neighbor to look at Sue's standardized reading test to offer some advice. What law has Sue's teacher violated?

   A. The Federal Confidentiality Act of 1975

   B. No law was violated because teachers are government employees.

   C. IDEA law right to privacy

   D. Family Educational Rights and Privacy Act (FERPA)

2. Noam Chomsky is known for what psychological idea?

   A. People have a predisposition to acquire language.

   B. Children who come from impoverished backgrounds are more likely to have behavioral and emotional difficulties.

   C. Whole-word reading is innate.

   D. Most male students are visual learners.

3. A school board wants to adopt a new but controversial math curriculum. As a school psychologist, you are called in for consultation. What do you tell the school board is best practice?

   A. There will be resistance from some parents, but most parents are looking to the board for leadership, so any decision must be final.

   B. Concerned parents need a way to voice their thoughts during the adoption phase.

C. The board needs to have an absolute consensus because everyone must agree on such an important issue.

D. The board needs to use curriculum experts to make informed decisions.

4. Which type of goal setting is most appropriate when teaching teenage students?

   A. Moderate goal setting within the Zone of Proximal Development

   B. Mastery goal setting to decrease anxiety

   C. Performance goal setting based on classroom norms

   D. High goals and standards to keep students striving for achievement

5. Which brain chemical is largely implicated in depression?

   A. Melatonin

   B. Serotonin

   C. Neuropeptides

   D. Endorphines

6. You are asked to perform an emotional assessment on a child who is withdrawn. Your first thought is to check for depression. What is the most appropriate tool to use in your assessment?

   A. The BASC

   B. The Vineland

   C. The Clinical Scales of Depression in Children

   D. The Beck Depression Inventory

7. A child you recently assessed with the Differential Ability Scales (DAS-II) had an overall standard score of 85. The student's Vineland survey from the teacher showed a standard score of 63, and the parent's Vineland resulted in a standard score of 87. You determine that the discrepancy between the adaptive assessment scores is most likely due to:

   A. Measurement error inherent in all tests

   B. The child behaves differently in different settings

   C. The subjectivity and different perceptions of raters

   D. The difficulty associated with completing complex surveys

8. One of the most effective interventions for a child with ADHD is which of the following?

   A. Placing him or her near the front of the classroom

   B. Increasing the student's self-awareness and knowledge of the disorder

   C. Having the student exercise before school to drain hyperactive energy

   D. Consistently reminding the student to take his or her medication (e.g., Ritalin, Adderall)

9. A 10th grade teacher has a visually impaired student who is given an extensive assignment. In this case, how should the teacher proceed?

   A. Allow other students to help the impaired student.

   B. The teacher should set aside a special time to discuss optional modifications of the assignment with the student.

   C. The visually impaired student should not be required to complete the entire assignment due to his or her handicapping condition.

   D. The task should be assigned as a joint effort between the teacher's assistant and the visually impaired student.

10. You are given a new cognitive assessment to administer for which you have no formal training. The parents of a student you will be testing are strongly requesting that you give their son the new test. From what you have read and heard from colleagues, the new test is highly regarded. What should you do in this situation?

    A. Ethically, you cannot administer the test and must use a more familiar test.

    B. You should practice with the test and administer it with supervision.

    C. You need to refer the case to another colleague who has administered the test.

    D. Ask a colleague to give the test, but be present during the administration.

11. Your assistant principal notifies you that a seventh grade student has made drawings depicting death. When asked why she drew such things, the student stated she thinks people who commit suicide are cool. After intervening and speaking with the student, what should you do next?

    A. Immediately notify the parents of this situation.

    B. Call the police and local suicide hotline for assistance.

    C. Notify social services and the school social worker.

    D. If the assessment shows the student is not in danger, make a note in the student's file and closely monitor the situation.

12. You have just completed a comprehensive assessment that took several days. The student you tested has a low IQ score and is considered low functioning. The student wants to know about his performance and asks you to explain your results. What is best practice in this situation?

    A. Tell the student that the test results gives you information on how he learns. The details should not be disclosed.

    B. Be truthful but brief with the student when you discuss the results.

    C. Secure permission from the parents before discussing assessment findings.

    D. Discuss the results with both the student and teacher at the same time.

13. You work in a community where many parents use illegal drugs. You are concerned about one particular elementary school that you spend 2 days a week servicing. You have heard students talk about drugs and wanting to use drugs. What is an effective intervention in this case?

    A. Talk to individual classes about drug abuse.

    B. Start a schoolwide antidrug campaign.

    C. Teach teachers how to talk with students about drugs.

    D. Gather parental, school, and community support to raise awareness and address the drug problem at school.

14. What memory technique should students use to remember a long series of numbers?

    A. Chunking

    B. Writing the numbers on paper

    C. Repeating the number series rapidly

    D. Teaching students to look for number patterns

15. According to the information-processing model, incoming information is encoded into what first?

    A. Long-term memory (LTM)

    B. The temporal lobe of the brain

    C. Conditional stimuli buffer

    D. Short-term memory (STM)

16. Diane is a sophomore at a large public high school. At the beginning of the year, Diane felt bullied by Sally. The principal quickly intervened and stopped the bullying. Now, at midyear, Diane reports to the administration that Sally is once again making unpleasant comments. This time the principal suspends Sally for 2 days and calls Sally's parents. What additional advice do you provide to the principal?

    A. Call Diane's parents to notify them of the situation.

    B. Make sure Diane has mental health support if needed.

    C. Have Diane talk with the school psychologist or social worker about how to deal effectively with harassment in the future.

    D. Have Sally sign a contract that outlines the terms of appropriate future behavior. The contract is necessary for re-admittance to school.

17. Your school district asks you to review a new cognitive assessment. While reading the technical manual you notice that the 1-year test–retest reliability coefficient is .77. You also make a note that the new test was correlated with

a well-known test to determine convergent validity. The convergent correlation coefficient for the two tests was .60. You can tell your district:

A. The new test has acceptable reliability and validity.

B. The new test's reliability coefficient supports the idea that the test measures what it is designed to measure.

C. The correlation between the new and old tests shows a modest association but it cannot be considered strong enough to recommend the using the new test.

D. The new test should be used by the district.

18. Metacognition refers to what?

A. Knowledge and self-awareness about one's own thoughts and abilities

B. A useful reading technique

C. A psychoanalytic counseling method used to help students think about their abilities and subsequent choices

D. The ability to activate prior knowledge when trying to make a reading passage meaningful

**Case example for questions 19–20:** Seth is a ninth grade student with an SED (significant emotional disability) label. He has several clinical disorders including ADHD and bipolar disorder. During the school day, Seth is able to control most of his behaviors but not all.

19. Despite Seth's above-average cognitive abilities, his grades are not stellar. However, he is passing all classes with Cs. Seth's teachers think he would benefit if he had more self-contained special education classes. What would you advise his teachers?

A. Tell his teachers to keep data to track Seth's progress. The data will be used during his next annual review IEP meeting to change his placement.

B. Tell the teachers that Seth's placement should be in the least restrictive environment and a more contained placement may not be warranted.

C. The special education team should discuss the issue with Seth's parents and then move him into more supportive classes once parental permission is secured.

D. Ask the parents what they want in this situation.

20. Seth's parents are very upset that he is making mostly Cs. Even though he is receiving special support services, his cognitive scores suggest that he should be making very high grades. The parents are threatening to file a lawsuit if Seth is not assigned increased para-educator time to address his needs more thoroughly. What most likely will happen in this situation?

A. The school is providing a "reasonable" education and does not have to supply all services. Therefore, the lawsuit will likely be unsuccessful.

B. The high cost of going to court will most likely force the school district to grant the parents' wishes.

C. The parents and school district know that an IEP is a legal document and once a child is receiving special services, he is entitled under federal law to be provided all services.

D. The parents will have to go to arbitration before a lawsuit can be filed.

21. You have administered the Cognitive Assessment System (CAS) to evaluate a student's cognitive functioning. The student's overall (general) standard score is 50. How do you interpret this score?

A. The student's performance is considered average given the range of scores is 1 to 100.

B. The student's score is roughly 2 standard deviations below average.

C. The student most likely has a significant learning disability.

D. The student's performance falls within the intellectual disability (ID) range of standardized scores.

22. What is the approximate age range for the Wechsler Intelligence Test for Children, Fourth Edition (WISC-IV)?

A. 5 to 16 years of age

B. 3 to 16.5 years of age

C. 5 to 17 years of age

D. 6 to 16.11 years of age

23. Rational–Emotive Therapy (RET) is founded upon what hypothesis?

A. That people's difficulties and problems stem from the choices they make. To change behavior, a therapist examines the individual's clarity of thinking and faulty beliefs.

B. A person's behavior is maintained by consequences.

C. Behavior is embedded in a dynamic environment. To change behavior, one must consider the individual's family, peer relations, and emotional needs.

D. Behavior is driven by unconscious drives to ease anxiety and to be accepted unconditionally by peers.

24. School "readiness" is related to which of the following?

A. A condition that exists when maturation is sufficiently developed to allow the rapid acquisition of basic academic skills.

B. When a child is able to control his or her behavior, he or she can attend school.

C. This is a term used to illustrate that a student is ready to advance to the next grade level.

D. A student is considered in a state of "readiness" when that child is focused and attending to auditory and visual information.

**25.** On a cognitive assessment, a student has a 15 standard score difference between the verbal domain and nonverbal domain. The full-scale score is a standard score of 95. How would you interpret the student's assessment if the child had a suspected reading problem noted by his teacher?

    A. The split between scores is significant but not necessarily clinical.

    B. It can be safely stated that the child has a learning disability.

    C. The full-scale score is invalid and cannot be used.

    D. It is considered best practice to administer a different cognitive test due to the difficulty interpreting scores with such variations.

**26.** When using standardized cognitive tests in students from diverse cultural backgrounds, it is important to remember which of the following?

    A. Some children are late bloomers and therefore IQ tests are not reliable for children younger than 6 years of age.

    B. Assume that a child's cultural background can mask her true abilities, which may not be fully illustrated on many IQ tests.

    C. Minority populations are over-represented in special education classrooms.

    D. Cognitive assessments should not be used with minority groups due to psychometric norming difficulties.

**27.** When observing students, which type of bias should psychologists consider a confounding factor?

    A. The halo effect

    B. Observer bias

    C. Subjectivity Principle

    D. Objectivity Principle

**28.** Curriculum-based measurements (CBM) are used for what purposes?

    A. CBM measures a school's progress toward explicit academic standards.

    B. CBM is especially effective when used to evaluate a teacher's skills.

    C. CBM measures a sample of a student's work over time to determine if an instructional method is effective.

    D. CBM is a measurement and assessment method that will most likely supplant standardized testing because it is considered an authentic tool.

**29.** Which brain structure is usually associated with emotions?

    A. Parietal lobe

    B. Broca's area

    C. Left frontal gyrus

    D. Amygdala

**30.** You are treating a student who is shy and unassertive. What is the most effective therapeutic approach in this case?

A. Rational–Emotive Therapy (RET)

B. Person-Centered (Rogerian) Therapy

C. Cognitive-Behavioral Therapy that uses modeling and rehearsal

D. Behavior therapy that rewards assertive behaviors

**31.** A school psychologist's duties are not solely devoted to special education students. When you are asked to counsel and/or assess the emotional state of a student by a teacher or parent, it is best practice to do what first?

A. Although a student may not be a danger to himself or others, a school psychologist should always meet with any student who needs counseling.

B. A psychologist should secure written permission from the parents to perform therapeutic and diagnostic services.

C. Although important, it is not mandatory to secure permission to meet with students because such services are free to all public school students.

D. School psychologists have a license or certificate from the state in which they work. Therefore, a psychologist can counsel students because to do so falls within the scope of his or her licensed duties.

**32.** You are asked to consult with a teacher regarding a classroom management problem. What is the best approach?

A. A nonhierarchal collaborative model should be followed.

B. A client-centered model is usually most effective.

C. A cognitive-behavioral consultation model typically produces effective results.

D. The ecological model is the most modern approach in this case.

**33.** Jack is a second grade student who struggled academically last year. He is not a behavioral problem and he is somewhat reticent in class. At the end of the current school year, the parents are thinking that Jack should repeat the second grade because his grades are still very low. How would you advise Jack's parents?

A. Interventions should be tried first and their effectiveness documented. Retention is typically not an effective strategy.

B. Jack, his parents, and teachers should be given the Light's Standardized Retention Scales to help determine if he should be retained.

C. Talk with Jack's parents and teachers about assessing him for special education services.

D. Jack's parents should be told that retaining a student, although very difficult for the parents, is usually an effective means of helping the student in the long term.

34. Which cognitive assessment is best suited for deaf students or students who do not speak English?

    A. The Differential Abilities Scales (DAS)-Nonverbal

    B. The WISC-IV with an interpreter

    C. The Universal Nonverbal Intelligence Test (UNIT)

    D. The Cognitive Assessment System (CAS)

35. For which disorder is flooding or "in vivo" therapy associated?

    A. Phobias and anxiety

    B. Depression and withdrawal

    C. Bipolar disorder

    D. Attention deficit hyperactivity disorder

36. According to Erikson, children in second grade are negotiating which stage of development?

    A. Initiative versus guilt

    B. Industry versus inferiority

    C. Peer pressure to conform

    D. Attachment to teachers and respect for authority

37. When implementing a crisis intervention for an off-campus suicide, the second step is to do which of the following?

    A. Dedicate a memorial

    B. Speak to classes about the deceased student

    C. Have a school assembly

    D. Plan to have a brief service at school to show respect for the deceased student

38. The NASP recommends that school psychologists should directly supervise no more than how many interns at one time?

    A. Two

    B. Three

    C. Four

    D. Eight

39. Which law requires that all children be identified for special services by school districts?

    A. Section 504 of the Civil Rights Law

    B. Free and Appropriate Education Act of 1977

    C. Individuals with Disabilities Education Act (IDEA)

    D. The Hohnbaum Amendment

**40.** Which of the following is considered the first intelligence test made for children?

    A. The WISC-I

    B. The Standford-Binet

    C. The Bellevue Test

    D. The Scholastic Aptitude Test-Alpha Series

**41.** Projective tests (e.g., Rorschach, Draw a Person) are usually used for?

    A. Building rapport with a student

    B. Gathering supplementary information about a student

    C. Determining if a student is prone to malingering and deception

    D. These tests should never be used in schools due to poor reliability

**42.** Parental complaints regarding Section 504 should be directed to which authority?

    A. The Department of Education

    B. The school district's administration office

    C. The Office of Civil Rights (OCR)

    D. The state's Board of Education

**43.** What is the primary difference between achievement tests and cognitive tests?

    A. Intelligence tests are norm referenced.

    B. Achievement tests are generally broader in content than intelligence tests.

    C. Cognitive tests are typically used to predict future learning more than achievement tests.

    D. Cognitive tests use standard scores, whereas achievement tests use grade-equivalent scores.

**44.** You find out that another school psychologist has violated an ethical rule. What should you do first?

    A. Attempt to talk with the person directly and address the situation informally.

    B. Immediately report the situation to school officials because you have an ethical obligation to do so.

    C. Notify the school psychologist that if he or she does not report the violation, you will have to report it.

    D. Not all ethical violations are legal violations. Legally, you do not have to take any action.

**Case example for questions 45–46:** A student was referred to you due to his behavioral disruptions in class. After a series of interventions, the special education team and parents agree that formal assessments should be initiated. The results from your formal cognitive assessment demonstrated that the student has a very large verbal and nonverbal difference between scores. Other streams of information support the contention that the student has a learning disability, specifically a nonverbal learning disability.

45. The parents have difficulty accepting your findings and demand to see the test protocol. Your response should be to:

    A. Show the protocol to the parents and give them a copy if they request it.

    B. Refuse to let the parents examine the protocol citing copyright laws and the need to keep testing material strictly confidential.

    C. Provide the parents with qualitative information and your reasoning when interpreting the test results. The protocol may be used in your explanation but not copied.

    D. Reiterate for the parents that the identification of a learning disability is a team decision and multiple pieces of information were used in the determination. After your explanation, supply the parents with all the necessary scores.

46. After a lengthy explanation, the parents in the above example are still refuting your results and want outside (private) testing done. Which of the following statements is most true?

    A. The parents can have a private assessment done at the school district's expense if they complete the formal appeals process.

    B. Parents can have a private assessment completed, but the school district is not obligated to pay for outside testing if the results are congruent with the school's assessments.

    C. Private assessments are never paid for by a public school district.

    D. Only a judge can order private testing that is paid for by a school district.

47. A high school student is in your office requesting to see you. He is visibly upset because of a serious fight he had with his girlfriend last night. You do not have permission to counsel him. What is "best practice" in this situation?

    A. You are not allowed to counsel a student without parent permission.

    B. It is acceptable to perform a brief intervention in an emergency or crisis situation.

    C. Refer the student to his counselor at school.

    D. Have the student wait in a supervised room until his parents can be contacted.

**48.** At what point in a counseling relationship do you explain the limitations of confidentiality?

A. During your initial meeting

B. After a solid rapport has been established

C. When your sessions with the student are nearing completion

D. If the student asks what will be disclosed to her parents

**49.** A parent and teacher complete an adaptive scales survey (Vineland) on a child suspected of having a cognitive impairment. The parent's version is significantly different than that of the teacher's version. What do you do?

A. The results are said to be invalid and another type of survey should be administered.

B. You should call the parent and teacher and ask questions regarding the survey. Ask about the child's functioning at home and school.

C. Analyze and use other assessment sources for your evaluation instead of the survey. Although not used in your evaluation, you must make a notation in your report as to why the survey was not used.

D. Interpret both the teacher and parent surveys separately and present the objective results to the special education team.

**50.** The stay-put rule is implemented at what time?

A. When due process has started

B. When due process has completed

C. The stay-put rule was eliminated with the revised IDEA of 1997

D. When it has been determined that a behavior was a manifestation of a child's disability

**51.** At what type of meeting are eligibility requirements discussed and interventions or modifications are reviewed?

A. During the initial staffing meeting with parents and the team

B. During the initial referral meeting

C. During the student's annual meeting

D. During the assessment and testing phase

**52.** When is it considered best practice to perform a student evaluation?

A. During the student's typical school day

B. When the child is on the playground, in order to see his true behavior

C. After you have examined authentic work samples and observations.

D. Research has demonstrated that midmorning is the most effective time

**53.** The consumption of large amounts of alcohol during pregnancy can cause?

    A. Mental retardation (MR)

    B. ADHD

    C. A host of childhood mental illnesses

    D. Fetal alcohol effects (FAE)

**54.** Autism is associated with which of the following?

    A. Pervasive developmental disorder (PDD)

    B. Obsessive-compulsive disorder (OCD)

    C. Leading cause of mental retardation

    D. Genetic disorder that is also linked to the X chromosome

**55.** According to Sattler and Kaufman, the most valid and reliable score(s) on mainstream intelligence tests, such as the WISC, is usually which score?

    A. The major cluster or domain score

    B. The individual subtest scores

    C. Ipsative score

    D. The global or full-scale standard score

**56.** According to educational theorists, when fostering intrinsic motivation you should use:

    A. Variable reinforcement

    B. Tangible rewards

    C. Verbal praise

    D. Choice selection

**57.** Typically, block design subtests on major cognitive assessments mostly evaluate the functioning of the:

    A. Right hemisphere of the brain

    B. Left hemisphere of the brain

    C. Both hemispheres of the brain

    D. Cerebrum

**58.** If a student's misbehavior increases after the teacher takes away his recess time, this is called?

    A. Spontaneous negative increase

    B. Response cost

    C. Negative reinforcement

    D. Punishment

**59.** High school students who have dysgraphia should be given what type of accommodation and/or modification on tests?

    A. Extra time

    B. Frequent breaks

    C. Multiple-choice tests

    D. A split-half version of the test

**60.** Which therapeutic method or therapy works best for selective mutism?

    A. Reality therapy

    B. Cognitive therapy

    C. Stimulus fading

    D. Flooding

**61.** A second grade teacher uses the removal of a desirable activity, such as music class, to shape the behavior of his special education students. The teacher does not think other interventions are practical or effective. As the school psychologist, how should you respond?

    A. The welfare of the student comes first and the school psychologist has a duty to report the teacher to the principal.

    B. It should be explained to the teacher that the method he is using might be working, but will most likely produce short-term results if no positive reward is used for compliant behavior.

    C. The teacher should be commended for finding something that works. Suggest that feedback should be given to the students when possible.

    D. Tell the teacher that he is making the students resentful and that he is fostering external instead of internal behavioral regulation in the student.

**62.** In regards to the regulation and guidelines for school psychology, a primary difference between the APA (American Psychological Association) and the NASP is that

    A. The NASP is the only accreditation body for psychologists.

    B. The APA does not endorse master or specialist level school psychologists.

    C. There is no difference between APA and NASP guidelines.

    D. The APA only regulates psychiatrists working in schools.

**Case example for questions 63–65:** You have completed a comprehensive battery of standardized tests on a student who was referred for special education services. Parents signed permission for your team to complete testing. After the staffing meeting, the parents' lawyer demands that you supply them with copies of your protocols.

**63.** As a licensed school psychologist you should do which of the following?

    A. Supply all the necessary copies so you are in compliance with federal law.

B. Discreetly state that all necessary information is in the IEP report and review the IEP with the parents.

C. You review the protocols with the parents but you do not have to make copies.

D. Call the school district's lawyers and have them speak to the parents.

64. Which specific law or case law requires parental access to records?

   A. IDEIA

   B. *Kramer v. Kramer*

   C. *Brown v. Board of Education*

   D. FERPA

65. If you copy protocols for parents or others, you might be violating what law?

   A. Federal copyright laws

   B. FERPA

   C. Fair Testing and Assessment Act of 1997

   D. IDEIA

66. Executive function primarily impacts?

   A. Cognitive planning

   B. Nonverbal learning

   C. Spatial reasoning

   D. Reading

67. Which is considered primary in crisis intervention?

   A. Leadership

   B. Community support

   C. Measured response

   D. Prevention

68. A teacher constantly sends his rowdy students to your office. By midyear, you are handling several students a week from this one particular teacher. You meet with the teacher in private to discuss the situation. You help him implement a behavioral management plan. Within a few weeks, referrals to you have dropped significantly. What consultation did you employ?

   A. A direct service model

   B. A consultee-centered service model

   C. A systems-based model

   D. The Caplan model

**69.** A student is referred to the school psychologist's office because he consistently makes inappropriate comments. What is your first approach to amending this problem?

 A. You figure out what is maintaining the behavior and stop the reinforcement.

 B. You set clear expectations for the student and enforce natural consequences.

 C. You perform a quick functional behavioral assessment (FBA) to determine the antecedent and consequence for the behavior so you can plan an intervention.

 D. You tell the teacher to write an office referral for the next incident so there is proper legal documentation.

**70.** Authentic assessments are different from standardized assessments in which primary way?

 A. Standardized assessments use statistics to compare a student to a norm group, whereas authentic assessments are more criterion based.

 B. Authentic assessments are considered informal methods.

 C. Standardized assessments are more time efficient.

 D. Authentic assessments are more time efficient.

**71.** According to many functional behaviorists, what are the primary reasons for most behavior?

 A. Attention, affiliation, and control

 B. Boredom, opportunity, and biological stimulation

 C. Stimulation, approval, and reinforcement

 D. Praise and approval

**72.** An upper elementary school student constantly makes poor grades despite his concerted efforts. According to Erik Erikson, if this student does not feel a sense of industry, he will develop problems involving:

 A. Shame

 B. Doubt

 C. Inferiority

 D. Role confusion

**73.** A sophomore will not break the rules of his school because he does not want to face the disapproval of his strict parents. According to Kohlberg, which stage of moral development is this student navigating?

 A. Preconventioal

 B. Conventional

 C. Postconventional

 D. Assimilation

Given a SEM of 6 points, what can be said of a student who receives a standard score of 90 on a cognitive assessment?

A. The student's range of scores is in the average to below average area.

B. The student has an average score.

C. The student has an upper borderline score.

D. The student's score is between the 84th and 96th percentiles.

**Case example for questions 75–76:** A seventh grade female student has a speech impediment and poor social skills. By the second month of school she is teased by a group of girls to the point at which the student becomes despondent. Several other students are aware of the teasing, but do not do anything about it. One day, the student writes a detailed note to her teacher that she will kill the teasing students if they do not stop.

**75.** In this situation, the school psychologist should do which of the following?

A. Immediately counsel all students involved.

B. Mediate the problem with the students involved in the situation.

C. Notify law enforcement immediately.

D. Warn all parents of the children involved in this situation about the threatening note.

**76.** In this scenario, a school psychologist should also do which of the following?

A. Seek to prevent a similar situation by instituting a schoolwide anti-bullying program.

B. Use an indirect consultation model to inform the principal about future options.

C. Conduct a formal survey to uncover potential future bullying and harassment problems.

D. Perform proactive interventions with identified bullies and suspend repeat offenders.

**77.** A student is referred to the school psychologist's office for negative self-talk. During the interview, you discover that the student believes she has always had bad luck and bad things just happen to her all the time. This student's belief is an example of:

A. Negative thinking

B. Internal locus of control

C. External locus of control

D. Low self-concept

**78.** A caring parent constantly completes homework for his daughter. Despite suggestions from teachers and school staff, the parent continues to complete assignments for his child. The parent in this situation is doing which of the following?

A. Instilling in the child a learned helplessness orientation

B. Undermining the child's self-concept and self-confidence

C. Breaking the law as outlined in the *Tarasoff* case

D. Modeling negative behavior

**79.** A teacher is in the community and sees one of his students at a store. The student has visible marks on his face and arms. The father of this child is known to be verbally aggressive and short tempered. The teacher should do which of the following?

A. The teacher is not legally obligated to notify social services because it is after work hours and not on school grounds.

B. The teacher needs to contact the school social worker immediately.

C. In private, the teacher should ask the student about the marks and then make an informed judgment whether to call social services.

D. As a mandated reporter, the teacher has a duty to notify social services about the marks.

**80.** A parent comes to you and demands that her son must be tested for special education services. The student has a history of poor grades and seems to daydream in class. What is best practice in this situation?

A. Suggest interventions before moving ahead with formal testing.

B. Start the assessment process because parents have legal rights to testing under IDEA law.

C. Tactfully tell the parent to have her son medically evaluated by a pediatrician for attention problems before formal school testing starts.

D. Inform the parent the law gives schools 60 days to complete testing.

**81.** When should a school psychologist suggest exploring more information regarding medication for ADHD to parents?

A. After all assessments have been completed

B. Never

C. Only after securing a release to speak with the student's pediatrician

D. When the student's behavior impacts other students

**82.** A student is asked to dial a phone number while hearing the number for the first time. This is an example of what type of process?

A. Short-term memory

B. Working memory

C. Information processing

D. Successive processing

**83.** A chief characteristic of Asperger syndrome is which one of the following?

A. Social skills difficulties

B. Delays in cognitive abilities

C. Inability to remember spatial and verbal information

D. Nonverbal learning disability

**84.** In regard to suspected child abuse cases, all school employees must do which of the following?

A. Notify the school administration of the suspected abuse.

B. Report cases of suspected abuse to police or social services.

C. Investigate abuse cases and follow up with police or social services.

D. Report abuse to the school social worker who is required to report abuse cases.

**85.** Traumatic brain injury (TBI) in children:

A. Can cause learning disabilities and attention problems

B. Is typically not as serious as adult TBI because a child's brain is more malleable than an adult's brain

C. In most cases will decrease the quality of life of children

D. Is reflected by significantly higher nonverbal than verbal scores on cognitive tests

**86.** During a formal assessment, you ask a child to say a word and then manipulate the word's sounds. What are you doing in this task?

A. You are testing for sound discrimination.

B. You are assessing word-sound fluency.

C. You are evaluating phonemic awareness.

D. None of the above answers are valid.

**87.** A teacher asks for your direct assistance regarding a disruptive student. You agree to observe the child. You discretely sit in the class and observe what happens before, during, and after the targeted behavior. Afterward, you determine that the student was acting out when the student was near a specific peer. What type of evaluation were you conducting to assist the teacher?

A. You were performing an FBA.

B. You were conducting a formal evaluation observation.

C. You were assessing antecedents and consequences.

D. You were evaluating the payoff for the student's behavior.

**88.** A student has significant difficulty perceiving and reproducing visual symbols accurately. An inability to perceive visual stimuli accurately is typically associated with which part of the brain?

A. Visual–spatial cortex

B. Parietal lobes

C. Frontal lobes

D. Occipital lobes

**89.** Cognitive psychologists hypothesize that the construct of "attention" can be categorized into different types. What are the primary types of attention?

A. Selective and fluent

B. Focused and fluent

C. Selective and sustained

D. Sustained and focused

**90.** When a preschool child imitates the aggressive behavior of an adult he has just seen in a movie, this behavior is based upon which psychological construct?

A. Modeling

B. Latent aggression

C. Observational learning

D. Behavioral dysregulation

**91.** Who is the theorist largely responsible for studying aggression in children and conducting experiments using a "bobo" doll?

A. B. F. Skinner

B. Albert Switzer

C. Albert Bandura

D. Carl Jung

**92.** A colleague asks you to review a journal article that describes several studies and experiments. You are specifically asked to discern the strongest correlation coefficient from the following. Which one depicts the strongest correlation?

A. .97

B. −.98

C. .100

D. −.250

**Case example for questions 93–95.** In an experiment, you want to examine the effect background music has on learning. You form two groups. One group studies with soft background music, whereas the other group studies in a quiet area.

**93.** The group exposed to background music is called the:

    A. Experimental group

    B. Independent group

    C. Control group

    D. Dependent variable

**94.** The group not exposed to background music is called the:

    A. Experimental group

    B. Independent group

    C. Control group

    D. Dependent variable

**95.** In the experiment, the music is considered the:

    A. Experimental variable

    B. Manipulation variable

    C. Independent variable

    D. Dependent variable

**96.** When you assess a student for special services, best practice suggests that you do which of the following?

    A. Use at least two valid standardized measures before identifying a disorder or disability.

    B. Secure a second opinion from another school psychologists before formally identifying a disorder.

    C. Use both valid formal and informal assessments to base your decisions.

    D. Do not use informal assessments.

**97.** Aphasia is normally associated with what type of problem?

    A. A speech or language disturbance

    B. A visual-motor disturbance

    C. An inability to read

    D. A difficulty with math or quantitative problem solving

**98.** A student employs a problem-solving strategy that reduces the number of options or alternatives to be considered. This student is using what type of problem-solving technique?

    A. Deduction

    B. Successive processing

    C. Logical reasoning

    D. A heuristic

**99.** A teacher asks you to assist with a student who has reading difficulties. You suggest that the student describe her reasoning and predict outcomes of selected paragraphs. Most likely, these suggestions are to improve the student's:

A. Reading fluency

B. Decoding skills

C. Comprehension skills

D. Encoding skills

**100.** During a structured interview, you notice that the interviewee is well groomed and has a quick but polite sense of humor. Care must be taken that your assessment results are not tainted by what psychological phenomenon?

A. Halo effect

B. Observer bias distortion

C. Perceptual-bias effect

D. Skalski effect

**101.** You work as a school psychologist for a rural school district. Budget problems and personnel shortages are persistent in your district. The principal of your school informs you not to make recommendations for parents to seek community counseling services for their children. Additionally, the principal informs you that you must only conduct group counseling sessions, not individual sessions. Based on ethics and best practices, how do you respond to this situation?

A. Given the practical concerns of the situation, you should comply with the principal's directives.

B. Explain your ethical obligations to the principal, but still comply with the directives.

C. Notify the principal that you cannot completely comply with the directives because some situations warrant certain actions that are ethical.

D. Consult with the district's attorney and bring the matter before the school board.

**102.** Curriculum-based measurement (CBM) enables a teacher to do which of the following?

A. Continuously monitor progress and adjust goals as necessary.

B. Compare a student's performance to the norm group to determine what is typical.

C. Provide evidence of teacher effectiveness in a given curriculum.

D. Determine whether a curriculum is reliable and valid.

103. When seeing a child for the first time in a counseling meeting, a school psychologist should first secure:

A. Consent from the principal or school administration

B. Informed consent from parents

C. Consent from the administration and parents

D. If licensed by a state government to work in public schools, no consent is necessary but is considered appropriate.

104. A school district is mandated to formally assess children of all ages with suspected disabilities. According to educational law, this previous statement is known as:

A. No reject

B. Child Find

C. Inclusion

D. Exclusion

105. Which standardized cognitive assessment is largely based on the Luria model and the PASS (Planning, Attention, and Simultaneous and Successive Processing) model?

A. The Differential Ability Scales (DAS)

B. The WISC-IV

C. Stanford-Binet-IV

D. The Cognitive Assessment System (CAS)

106. A counseling approach that embraces the idea that behavior is guided by one's self-image, subjective perceptions, and the need for growth toward personal goals is called

A. Psychodynamic counseling

B. Behaviorism

C. Humanistic counseling

D. Cognitive-behavioral counseling

107. The Cattell–Horn–Carroll (CHC) theory of intelligence forms the basis for many current cognitive tests. According to this theory, intelligence can be divided into domains such as which of the following?

A. Verbal–Nonverbal

B. Neurological–Cognitive

C. Cognitive–Behavioral

D. Fluid–Crystallized

**108.** NASP generally recommends how many school psychologists per student population?

    A. 1 per 1,000 students

    B. 2 per 1,000 students

    C. 1 per school

    D. 1 per 2,000 students

**Case example for questions 109–111:** An upper elementary school student is referred to the special team for unusual social and egocentric behavior. As a school psychologist, you first conduct an observation of the student and interview the teacher. Your inquiry reveals that the young boy has an uncanny ability to remember detailed facts about World War II military planes. You also find the child has motor clumsiness, abnormalities in inflection when he speaks, and difficulty in social situations. However, you note that he has a few friends and engages in group activities without external assistance.

**109.** Based on the presenting symptoms, you decide to formally test the student for which disability?

    A. Autism

    B. Nonverbal learning disorder (NVLD)

    C. Social processing disorder (SPD)

    D. Asperger syndrome

**110.** The parents have given you signed permission to help the student in the previous scenario. You decide that social skills training is the best initial approach. Which of the following best reflects social skills training?

    A. Self-awareness, positive reinforcement, and social praise

    B. Direct instruction, modeling, and coaching

    C. Metacognitive training, operant techniques, and active listening

    D. Perspective taking, response cost, and social praise

**111.** Your team feels that the student in this example needs special education services. In making the decision to offer the student special services, your team must demonstrate what critical finding?

    A. The child has a diagnosable disability as outlined in the *DSM-IV-R*.

    B. Your testing results must show a significant and verifiable processing deficit.

    C. The child's behavior has a significant impact on his social development and/or classroom performance.

    D. Standardized testing must document that the student has a score that is at least 2 standard deviations below the mean.

**112.** When conducting a behavioral observation, which of the following is critical to document and analyze?

    A. The frequency, intensity, and duration of the target behavior

    B. How many times the behavior presents itself when the antecedent is known

    C. The reinforcement of the targeted behavior

    D. The triggers for the behavior

**113.** According to the government (Centers for Disease Control and Prevention), approximately what percentage of the student population aged 3 to 17 has some form of learning disability?

    A. 2% to 3%

    B. 6% to 8%

    C. 12% to16%

    D. 15% to 20%

**114.** On common cognitive assessments such as the WISC-IV, what is the generally accepted full-scale standard score for gifted students?

    A. A standard score above 115

    B. A standard score above 120

    C. A standard score above 130

    D. A standard score above 150

**115.** A student who has a severe vision impairment is granted a school waiver that excuses her from taking the state's annual assessment test. The parents of this student demand that the school accommodate her so that she can take the test. According to the law, what is the school's responsibility?

    A. The school must fulfill the needs of the student so she can complete the standardized state test.

    B. The school is under no legal obligation but, ethically, should make the appropriate accommodations.

    C. The school should keep to its original plan and fully excuse the child from the test.

    D. The school's decision to spend resources to accommodate the student depends on whether the student has a 504 or IEP.

**116.** Which of the following statements regarding school violence is *not* true?

    A. There is a general profile of a "school shooter" that all school psychologists should know.

    B. Most perpetrators of school violence have been bullied in the past.

    C. Incidents of targeted school violence at school are rarely impulsive.

    D. Most attackers engaged in behaviors that caused concern in others.

**117.** The most effective intervention(s) for children with learning disabilities is which one of the following?

    A. Cognitive and behavioral

    B. Multifaceted or multimodal

    C. Linguistic

    D. Neuropsychological

**118.** The term "running record" is usually associated with which type of observational recording?

    A. Interval recording

    B. Narrative recording

    C. Event recording

    D. Ratings recording

**119.** What is the NASP's position regarding homeschooling?

    A. The NASP does not endorse the concept of homeschooling due to the lack of quality assurance and professional instruction provided to children.

    B. The NASP believes in collaboration between parents of homeschooled children and the public schools.

    C. Homeschooled children are most at risk for social developmental delays.

    D. Psycho-educational assessments should be used with caution with children who are homeschooled because they typically have a different learning style.

**120.** The ability to analyze and synthesize several pieces of information is related to which type of cognitive processing?

    A. Sequential

    B. Spatial

    C. Metacognitive

    D. Simultaneous

# Practice Test II

**DIRECTIONS: You have 2 hours to complete the following test. Be mindful to keep *strict* time limits. Although two answer choices might be true, select the one that is better. Do not leave any questions blank. If you change your answer, erase your previous choice thoroughly.** (Advice: Put a small check on those questions that are difficult to answer and move on to the next item. Remember to go back to the marked questions and complete them after going through all the questions and before finishing the test.) **Answers are provided following these tests.**

**Ready?**                                                     **Start Timing: 120 minutes**

1. Which one of the following responses is formal data *not* used in the RTI (response to intervention) process?
   A. To identify a student's learning problem or area of difficulty
   B. To target intervention strategies
   C. To help determine whether a student should be retained in a grade
   D. To decide whether interventions are related to positive student outcomes (effectiveness)

2. Interviewing is an important means to collect informal data. Which interview technique has a high degree of validity and allows for additional questioning?
   A. Semi-structured interview
   B. Structured interview
   C. Quasi-structured interview
   D. Unstructured interview

**Case example for questions 3–4:** As a school psychologist, you have a very busy work schedule. You receive several referrals for special education evaluations from parents and teachers. Your latest referral is a second grade student who has been formally referred for a special education assessment. The referral you received states that the young male student is well behaved, but he is struggling academically.

**3.** Given the previous situation, what would be your first step to address the referral?

    A. Call the parents to ascertain a developmental history.

    B. Talk to the teacher or primary referral source to better define the problem.

    C. Ask the RTI specialist what interventions have been employed.

    D. Review student records to ascertain how long the student has been struggling.

**4.** In this scenario, you talk to the teacher and she mentions the student is periodically off-task. However, the teacher cannot tell you when the student is off-task. You decide it is important to conduct an observation, but you are under time constraints. What observational technique is best in this situation?

    A. Interval time sampling

    B. Latency

    C. Comprehensive sampling

    D. Duration recording

**5.** Which analysis is *not* included in the three levels of an effective RTI data analysis?

    A. Analysis of the trend of the data

    B. Analysis of the level of the data

    C. Analysis of the quantity of data

    D. Analysis of the variability in the data

**6.** The pattern of change in a student's behavior *across time* can be best described as the

    A. Level

    B. Trend

    C. Variability

    D. Slope

**7.** You are analyzing RTI data that has been collected on a student's reading skills after the first 2 weeks of an intervention. You note that the data indicate variability, with scores very low one week but the next week the scores demonstrate significant gains. What is your initial response?

    A. The data is valid as students typically show variability with new interventions.

    B. The data is valid but should be interpreted with caution.

    C. The data is invalid and should not be used to make educational decisions.

    D. The data should be screened for confounding variables that are helpful to consider.

**Case example for questions 8–9:** Jack has been in a school's RTI process for math difficulties. Students in this process are ranked on a 1 to 5 scale, with 5 being the highest classroom benchmark and 3 being the aim line. Jack's data indicates that he scored a 2, 2, and 3 on the last three learning sessions. Also, Jack's level of response to the instruction is about 15% correct per data set.

8. In this situation, you should recommend to the teacher and support staff
   A. Focusing more effort on increasing the student's rate of correct responses.
   B. Modifying the instructions by providing better prompts, additional modeling, and corrective feedback.
   C. Considering significantly changing the instruction and intervention.
   D. Maintaining the intervention as the last data point shows a positive trend.

9. When examining data in this situation, which of the following does *not* need consideration?
   A. Is the percentage of correct responding below 85%?
   B. Are the data highly variable?
   C. Is the student from a low SES?
   D. Are there 2 to 3 consecutive data points that fall below the aim line?

10. During a special education evaluation, school psychologists are required to use which of the following items?
   A. Valid and reliable data
   B. Informal and formal sources of information
   C. Standardized and nonstandardized tests
   D. RTI and non-RTI data

11. You are asked to determine whether a child qualifies for special education services under the identification of intellectual disability (ID). You have already completed a cognitive assessment using the WISC-IV; which one of the following must you also complete?
   A. Woodcock-Johnson Test of Achievement
   B. Peabody Picture Vocabulary Test
   C. Vineland Adaptive Functional Test
   D. Berry-Buktenica Developmental Test of Visual-Motor Integration

12. What is the recommended guideline when collecting baseline RTI data?
   A. There should be no new highs (spikes) or lows for 3 consecutive data points.
   B. You should collect student baseline data for at least 1 week.
   C. 85% of your baseline data should be at least 15% below the class average.
   D. 15% of your baseline data should be at least 85% below the class average.

**13.** Which brain-based process is considered a basal neurological process that can be assessed with a neuropsychological test.

    A. Nonverbal reasoning

    B. Verbal reasoning

    C. Visual–spatial reasoning

    D. Processing speed

**14.** You are asked to perform a social and emotional assessment for a fifth grade student. Which procedures will be effective in your assessment?

    A. Give the BASC-II behavior assessment and the DAS-II cognitive assessment

    B. Give the Vineland-II adaptive functional assessment and conduct a student observation

    C. Conduct a functional behavioral assessment (FBA) and student interview

    D. Give the BASC-II behavior assessment and a functional behavior assessment (FBA)

**Case example for questions 15–16:** Sally is a third grade student who has difficulty with task persistence and work completion. She is respectful to staff and does not have a history of behavioral problems. Parents report that her father recently lost his employment and the family may have to move. Sally's teacher and mother have requested your assistance.

**15.** You decide to conduct an FBA on Sally to help inform a comprehensive intervention strategy. What are the initial steps in the FBA process?

    A. Interview the parents, perform an observation, formulate an intervention plan, and evaluate the plan.

    B. Define the problem, perform an observation, develop a hypothesis, and formulate a plan.

    C. Develop a hypothesis, perform an observation, consult with the teacher, and formulate a plan.

    D. Interview the teacher, perform an observation, develop an intervention, and evaluate the plan.

**16.** In the previous scenario, you carefully craft an intervention plan that is based on your FBA results. Your data suggests that Sally is socially motivated and she enjoys socializing with her friends during class. Which of the following intervention strategies is endorsed as an effective first strategy to use?

    A. Implement a simple individually tailored response cost plan.

    B. Employ an easy-to-use, point-and-level system.

    C. Modify the immediate environment to promote on-task behavior.

    D. Provide immediate corrective feedback for off-task behavior.

**17.** What is the primary difference between a curriculum-based assessment (CBA) and a curriculum-based measurement (CBM)?

    A. CBM is a term used to describe a specific type of measurement typically used for reading intervention programs in a RTI process.

    B. CBA is a term used to describe a broad assessment program or process, which may include CBMs or structured observations.

    C. A CBM is an assessment designed to measure the effectiveness of class-wide intervention programs.

    D. A CBA is designed to measure a student's progress in a remedial program.

**18.** Which of the following is the best example of a CBM?

    A. A student is given a nationally standardized test such as DIBELS. A standard score is derived and compared to national norms.

    B. A student is given a math test at the beginning of a semester, then given the same test at the end of the semester. Results are compared for growth.

    C. A student reads aloud for 2 minutes. The number of words read correctly and incorrectly are counted and compared to the class average.

    D. A student is given a classroom reading test and the results are compared to the state's standards for proficiency.

**19.** Generally speaking, a student might have an intellectual disability (ID) if the student has sub-average scores on an adaptive functional assessment and a standard score of _____ or below on a mainstream cognitive test battery.

    A. 85

    B. 80

    C. 75

    D. 70

**20.** You are asked to test a female student suspected of having a learning disability. The female student only speaks a few words of English, but she is fluent in Spanish. When you conduct your assessment it is prudent to do which of the following?

    A. When using an interpreter, the interpreter should be certified by the National Association of Interpreters (NAI) and speak both languages proficiently.

    B. If you use a cognitive assessment, only use assessments that are normed on a Spanish normative group.

    C. Use informal measures as well as appropriately normed assessments.

    D. Rely heavily on parent interviews, teacher data, and developmental history.

**21.** During a behavioral assessment, psychologists typically conduct student observations. What type of confounding factor should you be cautious of?

A. The halo effect

B. Subjectivity

C. Teacher bias

D. Thorndike effect

**22.** Although projective measures can be useful as part of a comprehensive assessment, many projective tests have been criticized for which of the following?

A. The need for the examiner to have extensive and specialized training to administer such tests.

B. The length of time to administer such tests is significantly longer than standardized tests.

C. Reliability, such as inter-rater reliability, is lower than standardized measures.

D. Projective tests are subject to confounding factors.

**23.** When collecting and analyzing data on student behavior, which three aspects of the target behavior should you emphasize in your analysis?

A. Intensity, variability, and duration

B. Intensity, duration, and frequency

C. Duration, quantity, and quality

D. Duration, frequency, and quality

**24.** A fourth grade student was referred to you due to overall low academic performance. In addition to RTI data and informal measures, you decide a full cognitive battery is appropriate. At the initial special education meeting, you meet with parents. What is best practice when you describe your WISC-IV results to the parents?

A. Start with interpreting the individual subtests, then add the global score.

B. Start with interpreting the global score, then add major subtests scores.

C. Only provide and interpret the global score.

D. It is generally good practice only to report below average scores.

**25.** You are asked to design a positive behavior support (PBS) plan for your school. Which one of the following PBS aspects is *not* an effective plan feature?

A. Establish and define clear and consistent expectations.

B. Acknowledge students for demonstrating the expected behaviors.

C. Use objective data to make decisions.

D. Staff should supervise students in all schoolwide areas.

**Case example for questions 26–28:** Bullying and harassment are major problems in schools. As a psychologist, you are asked to help mitigate bullying in your school.

26. One of the first steps you take to address bullying issues in your school is to educate your staff. When you present to staff you state that research indicates what percentage of students have reported being bullied?

    A. 50% to 60%

    B. 20% to 30%

    C. 80% to 90%

    D. 15% to 25%

27. Effective anti-bullying programs include all of the following except:

    A. Widespread staff supervision of students

    B. Programs to address bystander beliefs and behavior

    C. Strict consequences for bullying behavior and zero tolerance policies

    D. Systems to build social skills and to address social skill deficits

28. A student is caught harassing a group of students in a younger grade. You are asked to intervene. What is an effective approach to this situation?

    A. It is best to start individual counseling but maintain student confidentiality.

    B. Seek parental permission and then start group counseling.

    C. Recommend a restorative practice approach to the parents and administration.

    D. Recommend outside counseling to the parents.

29. When initially entering into a mental health counseling situation with a student, a school psychologist needs to carefully explain the limitations of confidentiality. When is it *not* appropriate to breach confidentiality with a student?

    A. When the student mentions that she wants to cut herself.

    B. When the student gives permission to breach confidentiality.

    C. When the student wants to damage property.

    D. When another psychologist engages in professional consultation.

30. Which type of counseling technique is generally referred to as best practice?

    A. Cognitive-behavioral therapy (CBT)

    B. Cognitive-emotional therapy (CET)

    C. Rational-emotive therapy (RET)

    D. Psycho-educational support (PES)

31. Schools generally favor behavioral techniques based on B. F. Skinner's theories. Which one of the following statements best describes Skinner's beliefs?

    A. Behavior is shaped by rewards.

    B. Behavior is influenced by a person's family environment.

    C. Behavior is shaped by consequences that follow the behavior.

    D. Punishment is not an effective means to modify behavior.

**32.** Jack is a ninth grade student participating in a program that requires him to assist students with Down syndrome. With supervision from the special education teacher, Jack tutors other students in their life skills curriculum and attends field trips to the store so the students can learn in the authentic environment. Which intervention strategy is being employed to help Jack build his empathy?

A. Behaviorism

B. Cognitive-behavioral therapy

C. Authentic environmental modification

D. Service learning

**Case example for questions 33–34:** You are working with a first grade student named Bill. Bill has a moderate level of autism and he is also suspected of having ADHD. Your current task is to teach him a classroom routine that involves several transitions. During your intervention, you conduct a task analysis and break the correct behavior down into multiple smaller steps. You follow a systematic instructional technique called DTI with several repeated trials in a highly structured environment.

**33.** In this situation, which behavioral technique are you following?

A. Applied behavior analysis (ABA) and intervention

B. Applied behaviorism

C. Discrete behavioral analysis and intervention

C. Strict behaviorism

**34.** Which one of the following choices is a key feature of ABA?

A. The use of positive reinforcers with prompts

B. Use of negative reinforcers only after positive reinforcement has been attempted

C. The use of prompts during the initial training stages, then gradual employment of fading techniques

D. The use of response cost techniques after desired behavior is taught

**35.** As a psychologist you will be consulted on crisis topics, plans, and interventions. Which one of the following statements is regarded as the best approach to crisis?

A. Crisis interventions should address individuals, groups, and systems.

B. Crisis prevention measures should be emphasized, developed, practiced, and put in place.

C. Postconvention measures should be rehearsed and considered part of a systematic response to crisis.

D. The building-level crisis team should always notify the district-level crisis team during a crisis situation for support and additional resources.

**36.** During a traumatic event, children may experience a wide variety of emotions and reactions. When actively intervening with children and staff who may have been exposed to a trauma or crisis situation, school psychologists should screen for what type of mental health issue?

   A. Contagion effects

   B. Posttraumatic stress disorder (PTSD)

   C. Depression disorder

   D. Anxiety disorder

**37.** A teacher alerts you to a high school student who has made suicidal comments during a class assignment. You meet with the student and decide a full suicide assessment is prudent. Given this situation, it is critical to do which of the following?

   A. Secure parent permission immediately before you start your student interview.

   B. Inform your school administrator that you are engaged in a priority assessment.

   C. Do not leave the student unsupervised during this process.

   D. Immediately notify the parent(s) that an assessment is underway, but you do not need parent permission to continue.

**Case example for questions 38–39:** You are a school psychologist practicing in an affluent public school district. You are notified by the district's crisis team that the most unfortunate situation has occurred. A seventh grade student died from a self-inflicted injury late at night. The next morning you are called to assist the crisis team at the student's school.

**38.** In the situation just described, your initial primary concern is which of the following?

   A. Your attention should be to support and provide resources for the student's family.

   B. It is critical to locate the student's friends and close peers within the school and provide them support.

   C. You must debrief staff before school starts.

   D. You must discuss and plan for contagion effects with school staff.

**39.** Which one of the following postconvention intervention strategies is valid?

   A. Provide students with verifiable facts and several details about the suicide to mitigate rumors.

   B. It is important to make a special early-morning public announcement to all students and staff to prevent rumors.

C. A special schoolwide assembly should be conducted to address contagion factors.

D. Provide in-school resources and counseling spaces for students who need additional support.

**40.** You are performing a formal evaluation on a 6-year-old student. During your teacher interview, the teacher mentions that the student has difficulty with simple symbolic thinking, which should have already started to emerge. According to Piaget, this student should be in which stage of development?

A. Preoperational stage

B. Concrete stage

C. Operational stage

D. Preconcrete stage

**41.** As a school psychologist, you will conduct evaluations on gifted and talented students. Recently, you have completed a full cognitive evaluation on a 15-year-old gifted student and will conduct a brief social and emotional assessment. As you interview the student, you find the student is opinionated and wants to follow a defined occupational path as a lawyer. According to Erik Erikson, this student is navigating which stage of development?

A. Adolescent versus preadolescent stage

B. Initiative versus shame and guilt

C. Identity versus role confusion

D. Industry versus inferiority

**42.** You are training school staff on the topic of school violence. A staff member asks you about the role of violent television shows and video games. Your response to the question is that you believe that children can learn violence and aggressive behaviors by watching violent movies. Your comments are based on research conducted by which psychological researcher?

A. Abraham Maslow

B. B. F. Skinner

C. Albert Bandura

F. Jean Piaget

**Case example for questions 43–46:** You are evaluating a sixth grade male student named Cameron for special education services. As part of your comprehensive assessment, you administer a full cognitive test battery (e.g., WISC-IV) and various social–emotional measures. The preliminary results are as follows. The full-scale standard score on Cameron's cognitive test battery is 113. All major cognitive domains were found to be within 2 standard points of each other. The BASC-II indicates that the teacher and parent forms both have T-scores of 64 within the Attention domain. Your semi-structured student interview reveals that Cameron follows the rules of the school, but he appears to follow these rules only to avoid punishment or gain rewards.

**43.** Given the previous scenario, what preliminary statement can you make about Cameron's overall cognitive ability?

    A. Cameron's standardized test score suggests that he might be gifted, but further information is needed to confirm this initial finding.

    B. Cameron's cognitive ability is considered solidly average.

    C. Cameron's cognitive abilities are considered low average.

    D. Cameron's cognitive abilities are situated within the high average to above average range.

**44.** Based on the provided BASC-II results, what is your initial impression regarding Cameron's attention?

    A. Cameron's attention scores are within the high average range and indicates he might have ADHD.

    B. Cameron's Attention BASC-II scores place him in the at-risk category for significant attention problems, but more information is needed to confirm this finding.

    C. Cameron's scores on the BASC-II are elevated slightly above normal and it is prudent to monitor his level of attention throughout the school year.

    D. Cameron's scores on the BASC-II are within the average range and both the teacher and parent forms confirm each other's observations in two environments.

**45.** In addition to the assessment tools used in the previous example, what other assessments should you complete in a comprehensive evaluation?

    A. A review of student records and student observation.

    B. A parent interview and behavioral checklist.

    C. A behavioral checklist and RTI data review.

    D. RTI data review and review of achievement test data.

**46.** In the previous scenario, in what Kolhberg stage of moral development is Cameron most likely situated?

    A. Preadolescent

    B. Conventional

    C. Preconventional

    D. Adolescent

**47.** As a school psychologist, you must discuss with parents a wide variety of behavioral and emotional disorders listed in the *Diagnostic and Statistical Manual (DSM)*. In one particular case, you have evaluated a student who has significant attention problems. Both formal and informal measures have indicated that the student you evaluated has difficulty sustaining his concentration and has been observed to fidget across multiple domains. During the parent meeting, you mention to the parents that their son has characteristics of ADHD. The parents want to know some research on ADHD. Which of the following choices is an appropriate research-based statement about ADHD?

A. You state that ADHD is diagnosed in approximately 15% of a school's population.

B. You respond by saying ADHD might be over-diagnosed, but the parents could benefit from a consultation with their pediatrician.

C. You state that school psychologists do not diagnose ADHD, but rather school psychologists identify student's with attention difficulties.

D. You state that ADHD is diagnosed significantly more in males than females.

**48.** For which of the following disorders is anxiety a prevalent characteristic in many cases?

A. Bipolar disorder

B. Personality disorder

C. Posttraumatic stress disorder

D. Mood disorder

**49.** Several years ago, autism spectrum disorders (ASD) used to have a prevalence rate of approximately 1 in every 2500 people. Current research indicates the prevalence rate for ASD has dramatically increased to which of the following levels?

A. 1 in every 186 people

B. 1 in every 55 people

C. 1 in every 1000 people

D. 1 in every 88 people

**50.** Deb was referred to your special education team for a full evaluation. The referral centered on Deb's below-average performance in reading and her lack of an age-expected response to reading interventions. While reviewing academic records and Deb's performance on the Woodcock-Johnson Test of Achievement, you notice that Deb struggles with quantitative concepts as well as reading. Due to your findings, it would be appropriate to screen Deb for which specific disorder?

A. Dyslexia

B. Dyscalculia

C. Intellectual disability

D. Specific learning disability

51. Landon is a seventh grade student suspected of having mild autism. When shown pictures of people engaging in various social interactions, you ask him how each person in the picture feels. Landon has difficulty with this task and provides atypical responses. This informal task provides information related to which theory?

    A. Theory of the Mind

    B. Theory of Perspective

    C. Theory of Subjectivity

    D. Theory of Objectivity

52. Students who have an external-locus-of-control perspective typically have difficulty in school and in life. An external locus of control is most closely aligned with which of the following?

    A. Display of helplessness

    B. Learned helplessness

    C. Behavioral problems

    D. Mood disorders

53. A teacher tells her class that they can have 10 minutes of free computer time to play recreational games if they complete their short math assignment first. What behavioral principle is this teacher employing to motivate her students?

    A. Proximal Development Principle

    B. Skinner Principle

    C. Premack Principle

    D. Principle of Positive Reinforcement

54. What is the primary difference between punishment and negative reinforcement?

    A. Punishment increases a desired behavior by decreasing undesired behavior, whereas negative reinforcement does not.

    B. Negative reinforcement increases behavior, whereas punishment decreases behavior.

    C. Negative reinforcement decreases all behavior, whereas punishment only decreases undesired behavior.

    D. Punishment and negative reinforcement are functionally the same terms.

55. Which of the following behavioral reinforcement schedules has shown to be effective, but it is difficult to modify the target behavior once established using this technique?

    A. Fixed-ratio reinforcement

    B. Mixed-ratio reinforcement

C. Variable-ratio reinforcement

D. Fixed-interval reinforcement

56. Several current mainstream cognitive test batteries are theoretically based and statically derived. What is the name of the modern psychometric test theory that includes such components as Gf (fluid intelligence) and Gc (crystallized intelligence), among others.

A. Thurstone Theory

B. Spearman Theory

C. Das-Naglieri Theory

D. Cattell–Horn–Carroll Theory

57. School psychologists typically consult with several educational specialists and must know some of the concepts and terms of other professional disciplines. In one situation, a school psychologist is told by a speech–language pathologist that a fifth grade student frequently makes grammatical mistakes in class. For example, during a conversation the student said, "To car we the go." The speech–language pathologist is concerned about the student's:

A. Semantic mistakes

B. Syntax

C. Phonological awareness

D. Phonemic awareness

58. Which theorist is associated with language acquisition and is known for using the term language acquisition device (LAD)?

A. Arthur Jensen

B. Mihály Csíkszentmihályi

C. Noam Chomsky

D. James Kaufman

59. A fourth grade teacher has been instructing her students in how to add and subtract fractions. Her self-made tests are based on classroom standards and mastery of a defined skill. What type of test is this teacher using?

A. Criterion-referenced tests

B. Norm-referenced tests

C. Local norm-reference test

D. Achievement test

Case example for questions 60–61: Michele is a student engaged in a school's RTI process. She is given assessments weekly to gauge her progress with reading comprehension. Michele's scores are based on a 1 to 10 scale, with a score of 10 being the highest score possible. Her scores for the past 2 weeks are 1, 5, 7, 7, and 10.

**60.** What is the mean score in the given set of numbers?

  A. 7

  B. 5.5

  C. 5

  D. 6

**61.** What is the mode in the given set of numbers?

  A. 7

  B. 5.5

  C. 5

  D. 9

**62.** You are asked to evaluate a new cognitive abilities screening test. In the technical manual, you notice the full-scale standard score of the new test has a statistical correlation of .68 with another well-respected cognitive test. Given these details, you can make which of the following assumptions?

  A. The new test has acceptable reliability.

  B. The new test has unacceptable reliability.

  C. The new test demonstrates an acceptable effect size.

  D. The new test shows convergent validity.

**63.** Brooke is a first-year psychologist practicing in a small affluent public school district. A struggling teacher is teaching at a new grade level and asks Brooke for a consultation regarding effective teaching practices. During her consultation, Brooke should *not* make which of the following statements to the teacher?

  A. Try activating students' prior knowledge before teaching new concepts.

  B. Provide corrective feedback during frequent practice sessions.

  C. Give additional homework items when new concepts are taught.

  D. Try to place new concepts within the students' zone of proximal development.

**64.** Student learning develops as targeted skills progress through phases. Which of the following processes is an accurate depiction of student learning?

  A. Acquisition → proficiency → generalization → adaptation

  B. Acquisition → practice → generalization → adaptation

  C. Acquisition → proficiency → application → adaptation

  D. Practice → proficiency → generalization → adaptation

**65.** Best practices in pedagogy involve which of the following broad concepts?

  A. Explicit and incremental approach to presenting information

  B. Explicit and systematic approach to presenting information

C. Repetition and practice of new information

D. Exposure and rehearsal of new concepts

66. An effective teacher is able to respond to the individualized needs and abilities of all learners in his classroom. Which of the following important teaching concepts is the teacher using?

A. Small-group instruction

B. Student subjectivity instruction

C. Differentiated instruction

D. Cooperative learning

67. In addition to student motivation, school climate, and school policies, what is another factor in student success or failure?

A. Family involvement

B. Socioeconomic status (SES)

C. Poverty

D. Standardized curriculum

68. A middle school administrator calls the school psychologist into a conference with a student's parents at the end of the school year. The student in question has been struggling this year and has failed all classes. On state assessments, the student has scored significantly below the standards for her grade level. The parents are worried about moving their daughter to high school if she does not have the academic skills and she is not adequately prepared. What would be a good recommendation for the school psychologist to make?

A. Administer the Light's Retention Scale to see if the student qualifies for grade retention.

B. Recommend retention only in core subjects, but allow the student to attend elective courses at the high school next year.

C. Seek additional information to determine whether other factors are involved in the student's struggles.

D. Recommend summer school to make up for failed courses instead of grade retention.

69. Which of the following choices are *not* typically associated with zero tolerance policies?

A. Racial disproportionality

B. An increasing incidence of suspensions and expulsions

C. Elevated dropout rates

D. A decrease in behavioral problems

70. Cooperative learning is an effective teaching method. A chief benefit of cooperative learning is:

    A. Students increase their prosocial skills.

    B. Students increase their own learning skills by helping others and gain a greater understanding of individual learning differences.

    C. Cooperative learning techniques are more time efficient than other teaching methods.

    D. Cooperative learning increases sympathy as well as academic skills.

71. Although token economies are effective systems to use in behavioral modification programs, what is a complaint often stated by teachers regarding them?

    A. Token economies are too expensive.

    B. Token economies are generally only effective for elementary students.

    C. Token economies are sometimes cumbersome to implement.

    D. Token economies do not maintain the target behavior once withdrawn.

72. A teacher, who typically gives students large projects and assignments, asks the school psychologist for help with two struggling students. The students are well behaved and do well in other classes but have difficulty completing work in her class. The psychologist's observation and recommendation should include which of the following?

    A. A task analysis to recommend where to break larger tasks into smaller steps.

    B. A time interval observation and recommendation to the school's RTI process.

    C. The psychologist should review academic records first, then recommend a remedial program.

    D. A qualitative observation and recommendation to the school's RTI process.

73. A second grade teacher asks you to help with a student, named Amy, to develop her reading skills. The teacher stated that Amy is a fluent reader, but her comprehension is below her peers. Which comprehension reading strategy would you recommend?

    A. Linda-Mood-Bell Reading Intervention

    B. SQ3R

    C. Wilson Reading Remediation Program

    D. Woodcock-Johnson Reading Intervention

74. What is an example of an accommodation for a student who struggles with reading?

    A. Having the student point to pictures of answers instead of writing answers about an assigned reading text

    B. Having the student take a reading test that is more aligned with his level of reading

C. Allowing extra time for the student to read a text during assignments or tests

D. Allowing the student to read books at a lower grade level

75. According to cognitive-behavioral theorists, learning is supported by mental representations of new concepts merging with a person's existing mental concepts. In this example, existing mental concepts are called:

A. Subjective impressions

B. Neuro-cognitive representations

C. Imprints

D. Schema

76. When engaged in a professional consultation situation, which of the following personality traits are important elements for success?

A. Empathy and trustworthiness

B. Expertise and knowledge

C. Ability to set boundaries and professionalism

D. Efficient and respectful

77. When collaborating and consulting with other staff, psychologists should be mindful of all of the following considerations *except*:

A. Internalized coping styles

B. Personality traits

C. Intelligence

D. External coping styles

78. Which model of consultation focuses on building the teacher's skills to address student problems in the future?

A. Consultee-centered model

B. Student-centered model

C. Strength-based model

D. Client-centered model

79. You are asked to help address a kindergartener's difficult behavior. The teacher is new and you decide to address the problem yourself. You directly teach the student self-regulation skills. In this particular case, you are engaged in which type of consultation model?

A. Consultee-centered model

B. Student-centered model

C. Strength-based model

D. Client-centered model

**Case example for questions 80–83:** A first grade teacher asks for a consultation with you. The teacher is concerned about a student named Jack. Jack has difficulty interacting with his peers, teases the girls in class, and is frequently off-task.

80. In this example, you decide to call a meeting for all relevant parties such as the teacher, parents, and administrator. This type of special consultation is called a:
    A. Conjoint behavioral consultation
    B. Client-centered consultation
    C. Consultee-centered consultation
    D. Multisystemic consultation

81. During your consultation with the staff and parents, your first step is to do what?
    A. Collect data on the problem.
    B. Define the problem as specifically as possible.
    C. Ask what interventions have been already implemented.
    D. Review the student's records.

82. All of the following are common barriers to effective consultation *except*:
    A. Adversarial relationship with outside agencies
    B. Communication difficulties among parties involved in the consultation situation
    C. Unclear or unfocused goals
    D. Financial considerations

83. Of all the consultation models, which model is generally considered a best-practice model?
    A. Conjoint behavioral consultation
    B. Client-centered consultation
    C. Consultee-centered consultation
    D. Multisystemic consultation

84. When is it legal to disclose the confidential records of a student to a third party?
    A. When a medical doctor requests student records
    B. When your administrator provides you with written consent
    C. When you are ordered to do so by a police officer
    D. When the student may be in danger

85. You are a school psychologist fully employed by a large public school district. A portion of this school district is very wealthy. During the summer months when the schools are closed, a parent in your district asks you to

complete a full cognitive assessment on her sixth grade child. The parent needs a full-scale cognitive test score so she can register her son at a private school. The parent is willing to pay you for your service. What should you do in this situation?

A. Refer the parent to the school psychologist at the student's home school.

B. A psychologist can accept this work if she is licensed and qualified to do so as a private practitioner.

C. Inform the parents that the service she seeks is provided free of charge by the public school district her son attends.

D. A school psychologist cannot accept this type of work.

**86.** What is the appropriate number of interns that a supervisor (i.e., PhD-level psychologist) can oversee?

A. 1

B. 20

C. 10

D. 5

**87.** Jackie is a school psychologist who has been practicing for 3 years. She shares a job with another psychologist named Mike. Jackie recently discovered that Mike has been giving money to other staff for referrals to his private counseling practice. Many of the students Mike counsels for a fee are regular education students at the high school. What should Jackie do in this situation?

A. File a grievance with NASP's ethical board.

B. Inform the school's administrator.

C. Discuss the situation with Mike directly and file a grievance if the practice does not cease.

D. Notify the parents that counseling services are provided for free by the school.

**88.** When a formal ethical complaint is filed against an NASP member, the NASP can take several potential actions. Which one of the following actions is *not* valid?

A. Expel the member from the NASP.

B. Require the member to seek additional training and skill building.

C. Require the member to provide a formal apology.

D. Revoke the license of the practitioner.

**89.** Aversive behavior modification techniques are legal in many states. What is considered best practice regarding aversive techniques such as restraining and suspensions?

A. It is best practice not to employ aversive techniques in any situation.

B. Aversive techniques should only be employed as a last resort.

C. It is best practice to use aversive techniques only if such techniques comply with strict state laws and regulations.

D. It is best practice to use aversive techniques on a case-by-case basis.

90. During a confidential counseling situation, a high school student informs you that his uncle uses illegal drugs. The uncle does not live with the student, but visits the student monthly. What should you do as the school's psychologist?

A. You should ask the student more questions to determine whether the student is in danger.

B. You should immediately notify law enforcement.

C. You should consult with social services, without using names, to secure guidance about what you should do and to stay in compliance with local laws.

D. You are not required to do anything other than provide support for the student.

91. A student receiving special education services brought a knife to school. He claims that he forgot that he had the pocket knife in the backpack, which he had taken on a fishing trip with his father. The student was suspended for 10 days. What violation of this student's rights occurred?

A. A special education student cannot be removed from school for more than 10 days.

B. A special education student cannot be suspended for more than 7 consecutive days.

C. A special education student must have a special review meeting if suspended 10 days or more.

D. Special education students cannot be expelled or suspended for more than 10 days, but they can be enrolled in a school that better addresses their needs.

92. A student is receiving special educational services for a mild dyscalculia disability. The special education team leader has placed this student in classes designed for students with significant math needs. The special education teacher reasons that it is better to "over serve" a student with mild needs than it is to under serve such students. In this case, which legal aspect of special education law does the teacher run the risk of violating?

A. Over spending federal funds on students with lesser needs

B. Least-restrictive environment

C. Least needs clause of IDEA law

D. Least needs clause of Family Education Rights and Privacy Act (FERPA) law

93. Which law mandates that schools must keep strict and confidential records?

A. IDEA of 2004

B. Federal Education Confidentiality Law of 1974

C. FERPA

D. IDEA Improvement Act of 2008

94. According to the law, what is the primary difference between special education law (IDEA) and Section 504?

A. There is no difference as both laws essentially regulate services for people with disabilities.

B. Section 504 is only for students who have physical disabilities, not learning disabilities.

C. Section 504 is for students who have handicaps diagnosed by medical professionals.

D. Section 504 was created by the Americans with Disabilities Act (ADA) and has a broader definition of disabilities than IDEA.

95. A parent of a sixth grade student is suing a school district because the school psychologist tested the student 3 years prior without parental consent. At the time of the initial evaluation, the psychologist called and left messages for the parent asking her to provide consent for the child's triennial review, but the parent never returned the calls. At a subsequent meeting, the parent was upset about the testing but allowed services to continue for another 2 years. What is the most likely reason the parent's lawsuit will not succeed?

A. The parents were informed of their rights at the meeting 3 years ago.

B. The student did not demonstrate harm from the services provided.

C. You do not need parental consent to test for triennial reviews.

D. The psychologist made documented attempts to contact the parents.

96. According to IDEIA, how much time does a special education team have to complete a formal evaluation if signed permission to proceed with an evaluation has been provided?

A. 45 days

B. 60 days

C. 30 days

D. 90 days

97. Although the roots of school psychology date back to the late 1800s, the first school psychologist was officially recognized in 1915. This psychologist also developed and used tests to measure development in children. Who was this pioneer of school psychology?

A. Arnold Gessell

B. B. F. Skinner

C. Carl Young

D. Charles Spearman

98. The field of psychology has grown increasingly more scientific since its origins over 100 years ago. Psychometric testing, which scientifically measures human traits, has helped to establish psychology as a legitimate discipline. Despite its roots in science, psychology is not without controversy. A famous psychological researcher, known for his work in behavioral genetics, was criticized for his assertion that intelligence has a strong genetic basis. Who was this famous psychological expert?

    A. Raymond Cattell

    B. Charles Darwin

    C. Philip Vernon

    D. Arthur Jensen

99. A school district has two curriculum tracks. One track is for college-bound students and one track is for vocational training. The vocational track is typically for students with limited financial means. This school district was sued because it violated the law by ability tracking students and denying access to college courses to some students. In the final legal decision, the judge based his opinion on which landmark case?

    A. *Diane v. State Board of Education*

    B. *Brown v. Board of Education*

    C. *Hobson v. Hansen*

    D. *Larry v. Riles*

100. A district-level school psychologist is asked to lead a threat assessment on a high school student. The student was caught at school with pepper spray and a list of students targeted for revenge. The threat assessment team was thorough during the inquiry and confidential student information was shared with the administration and law enforcement. Parents were not present during the assessment. Because a violent incident was averted and disciplinary action was taken against the student, the parents of the targeted students were not notified. What potential legal violation is involved in this situation?

    A. Since law enforcement was given confidential student information, FERPA may have been violated.

    B. A duty-to-warn infraction occurred.

    C. Informed consent by the parents was not secured prior to the threat assessment.

    D. A psychologist cannot conduct a threat assessment on a student without the student's parents or legal representation present.

101. What famous landmark case ruled that public schools could not segregate based on race? This law is also known as the antisegregation law.

    A. *Hobson v. Hansen*

    B. *Brown v. Board of Education*

C. *Rowley v. Board of Education*

D. *Larry P. v. Riles*

102. A student was in a car accident and sustained substantial damage to the left temporal lobe, especially to Broca's area. Given this information, it is reasonable to assume that the student may have difficulty with which of the following cognitive abilities?

A. Spatial reasoning

B. Sustaining focus

C. Auditory long-term memory

D. Expressive language

103. Neuropsychology is related to school psychology, but the primary focus of neuropsychology is which of the following?

A. Neuropsychology is concerned with brain–behavior relationships.

B. Neuropsychology focuses on the neurological aspects of intelligence.

C. Neuropsychology gives practitioners information that can be used to predict student achievement.

D. Neuropsychology evaluates a student's higher level reasoning and problem-solving skills.

104. Which of the following brain chemicals is thought to be implicated in producing positive moods and emotions, especially those associated with rewards? Parkinson's disease and ADHD are also associated with an imbalance of this neurochemical.

A. Serotonin

B. Dopamine

C. Endorphins

D. Cortisol

105. Cognitive-psychological researchers use the term "executive function" to describe a constellation of behaviors or functions necessary for success. School neuropsychologists are most likely to describe the same executive functions, such as initiation, impulse control, organization, and attention, by using which of the following terms?

A. Neurocognitive function

B. Frontal lobe function

C. Global neurocognitive function

D. Temporal lobe function

**106.** A child who has significant neurological impairments in the right hemisphere of the brain due to medical reasons would most likely have which of the following learning problems?

A. Difficulty with memory for previously learned skills

B. Phonological processing problems

C. Reading and spelling difficulties

D. Difficulty with new learning

**107.** The information-processing model, originally created by cognitive psychologists, helps practitioners conceptualize how humans think and learn. Which of the following choices best illustrates the cognitive processing model?

A. Input → processing → encoding

B. Encoding → processing → input

C. Input → processing → output

D. Attention → processing → output

**108.** A T-score of 65 is considered to be within which range?

A. Above average

B. Average

C. Below average

D. Significantly below average

**109.** Colette, a third grade student, has a documented history of reading problems. Colette's family is supportive of her learning, but they struggle financially and had to move twice in the past 2 years. The parents and teachers are worried that Colette will fall further behind in her reading development. In this situation, what should the school psychologist recommend?

A. The psychologist should recommend a special education evaluation based on the Child Find law.

B. The psychologist should recommend an after-school tutoring program and community support services.

C. The psychologist should make a formal recommendation to the school's RTI process.

D. The psychologist should consult with the student's team and parents.

**110.** You are counseling a second grade student who is significantly concerned about her father's recent unemployment. From Abraham Maslow's perspective, you could say this student is coping with the aspects found at which level?

A. Love and belonging

B. Safety needs

C. Self-actualization

D. Basic needs

**111.** Modeling and role playing are key intervention techniques for which type of problem?

A. Depression

B. PTSD

C. ADHD

D. Social skills deficits

**112.** You are consulting with a parent of a regular education high school student who has been caught using cocaine. The parent believes her son is distraught because he was denied admission to a selective university that he worked diligently to attend. You counsel the parent to discuss with her son that he may not be able to control the situation, but he has control of how he chooses to respond to the situation. Which counseling theorist emphasizes an individual's choice?

A. Viktor Frankl

B. Sigmund Freud

C. Carl Rogers

D. Abraham Maslow

**113.** In which of the following situations is the technique of time-out appropriate to employ?

A. When a child blurts out answers in class despite being told twice to stop

B. When a student with ADHD starts to have difficulty focusing on the task at hand

C. When a student is socializing during a test

D. When a student moves around the room without permission during a teacher's presentation of a new concept

**114.** In an RTI process, Tier 2 (Level Two) interventions are generally associated with which of the following?

A. Intensive interventions

B. Benchmark interventions

C. 5% to 8% of the student population

D. Strategic interventions for at-risk students

**115.** When conducting an ecological assessment, what four components should psychologists emphasize?

A. School environment, student records, formal assessments, and learning style

B. School environment, home environment, community environment, and social skills

C. Instruction, curriculum, environment, and learning style

D. Informal assessments, formal assessments, student records, and student interview

**116.** A parent is demanding that her son be placed on an IEP because he has a formal diagnosis of schizophrenia. The student's pediatrician has also recommended an IEP and wrote a prescription for one. Despite the mother's concern, the student's medication appears to be effective in managing his disorder and he is able to make educational progress. As a school psychologist, what is your response to the parent?

A. If there is no educational or social impact, then a formal special education IEP may not be appropriate.

B. Legally, a medical doctor's diagnosis and recommendation must be honored.

C. Although the school is not legally obligated to provide an IEP in this situation, it is good practice to provide special education support.

D. It is highly unusual not to provide an IEP to a student with schizophrenia and one should be provided to help the student in the future.

**117.** From a historical perspective, which is a new role for schools?

A. Reading interventionist for RTI programs

B. Brain injury resource specialist for school districts

C. Threat assessment consultant for schools and law enforcement

D. Autism evaluation specialist

**118.** What type of behavioral intervention would you recommend for a student with a phobia involving insects?

A. Flooding

B. Cognitive-behavioral therapy

C. Systematic desensitization

D. Functional behavioral analysis and intervention

**119.** According to neuro-cognitive research, students who sacrifice sleep to play hours of continuous video games might develop which of the following problems?

A. Antisocial personality disorder

B. Traits normally associated with ADHD–Inattentive Type

C. Aggressive tendencies and poor social skills

D. Difficulties with memory and learning

**120.** Before administering a new psychological assessment, it is reasonable for a school psychologist to do which of the following?

    A. Complete a formal training course on the new test.

    B. Give the new test to students but report the scores as informal measures until proficiency is achieved.

    C. Practice with the new test and be supervised by a colleague until proficient.

    D. Watch a training video on the new test.

# Practice Tests

## Answers and Explanations

## Practice Test I

**1. D.** FERPA law governs student information and confidentiality related to educational records. *Ethical, Legal, and Professional Foundations* domain.

**2. A.** Noam Chomsky is known for concepts related to language acquisition. *Applied Psychological Principles* domain.

**3. B.** During a consultation, people must have an avenue to express themselves and feel like their concerns are considered. *Consultation and Collaboration* domain.

**4. A.** It is critical to have high but realistic goals when teaching students. Educational goals need to be within a student's attainable limits, which is called the Zone of Proximal Development. *Research-Based Academic Practices* domain.

**5. B.** Serotonin is typically implicated in clinical depression. *Note:* There are several neurochemicals that are also associated with various disorders, but always choose the *primary* chemical when provided test choices. *Applied Psychological Principles* domain.

**6. D.** A well-known and mainstream instrument that measures depression symptoms and traits is the Beck Depression Inventory. *Data-Based Decision Making* domain.

**7. C.** This is a very difficult question to answer because other answer choices could be correct, but the *best* answer is C. Given the presenting facts of this case, it is unlikely a student would score over 20 standard points higher at home than at school because the inter-rater reliability is very good with the Vineland. You should first assume there may be a problem between the raters when scores are extremely discrepant. *Data-Based Decision Making* domain.

**8. B.** Although exercise and student placement in the classroom are effective interventions, raising a student's awareness of her difficulty is a key first step in treatment. *Research-Based Behavioral and Mental Health Practices* domain.

**9. B.** When students feel they have a voice in their own learning, they tend to perform better. Students with certain types of difficulties can complete full assignments and should not be denied the opportunity if there are accommodations that can mitigate a person's disability. *Research-Based Academic Practices* domain.

**10. B.** In practice and in real-world settings, it is permissible to study new tests and administer such tests with supervision or guidance from a qualified practitioner colleague. *Mixed* domains, but primarily *Data-Based Decision Making* and *Ethical, Legal, and Professional Foundations.*

11. **A.** It is best practice to share important information with parents about their children, even if further investigations suggest the issue is not life-threatening. Parents will have to be notified early in all cases of suicidal ideation. However, police or social services do not necessarily have to be notified in all cases. *Consultation and Collaboration* and *Research-Based Behavioral and Mental Health Practices* domains.

12. **C.** To prevent a difficult situation from developing, parental notification about cognitive assessment results should be secured first before talking with students about results. However, answer choice A is also a good response, but this statement is general enough that such a comment could be made before the assessment process starts to build rapport with the student. *Data-Based Decision Making, Consultation and Collaboration,* and *Ethical, Legal, and Professional Foundations* domains.

13. **D.** This question is one that seems easy to answer at first, but then you find all answers are correct. Your task, as mentioned earlier, is to find the *best* answer. In this case, the most encompassing answer choice is D because it covers items found in other choices. *Consultation and Collaboration* and *Research-Based Behavioral and Mental Health Practices* domains.

14. **A.** Chunking is a well-known psychological technique that is a common memory aid, such as when people memorize or repeat phone numbers. Phone numbers are a series of numbers broken up into chunks by hyphens so that they can be easily memorized. *Research-Based Academic Practices* and *Applied Psychological Principles* domains.

15. **D.** Straightforward factual answer. *Applied Psychological Principles* and *Research-Based Academic Practices* domains.

16. **A.** Legally, it is important to notify parents when aggressive actions are involved between students. All other answer choices are good responses and valid, but you must perform the actions provided in A. *Ethical, Legal, and Professional Foundations* domain.

17. **C.** Although there are slight differences of professional opinion about what is best practice related to validity and reliability cutoff coefficients, a test's psychometrics should be, in general, above .70. It is suggested by this author that test psychometrics be above .80. *Data-Based Decision Making* domain.

18. **A.** The definition of metacognition is defined by answer choice A. Note that choices B and C may also be valid responses based on their applied nature, but the best response for the definition is A. *Applied Psychological Principles* and *Research-Based Academic Practices* domains.

19. **B.** Least restrictive placement is a legal issue that must be honored if a student is making reasonable progress. Note that a student making Cs is considered reasonable academic progress. *Ethical, Legal, and Professional Foundations* and *Research-Based Academic Practices* domains.

20. **A.** As noted above, the LRE concept is a legal issue and should be honored. Students do not have to make the highest grades to make academic

progress and schools are not obligated to make sure students make the highest grades.

21. **D.** A standard score of 50 is significantly below average and suggests a high level of cognitive impairment. The new term used to describe significant cognitive difficulties is intellectual disability, which in clinical settings may still be referred to as mental retardation. *Data-Based Decision Making* domain.

22. **D.** The answer to this question is factual. While it is unlikely you will have such a specific question, some exams may have such an item. Students who answer such questions correctly are most likely well prepared to answer questions within this domain. *Data-Based Decision Making* domain.

23. **A.** Although RET is rarely employed in schools, components of RET are frequently used and helpful to school psychologists. One of the tenets of RET is that people's behaviors are driven by their beliefs. *Research-Based Behavioral and Mental Health Practices* domain.

24. **A.** School readiness is a broad term that encompasses both behavior and cognitive aspects of a child. Look for a key word association with the concept of school readiness, which is "maturation." *Applied Psychological Principles* domain.

25. **A.** Differences between scores are observed in the general population. Although such splits between scores should always be considered, it is important not to jump to conclusions. Follow-up testing to confirm the suspected disability and more information is warranted in the given situation. *Data-Based Decision Making* domain.

26. **B.** Although other choices are good responses, answer B is the best answer. Note that choice D is not a good choice and it is not accurate. Current cognitive assessments are better developed to account for cultural issues than previous assessments. Despite improvements, cultural issues are still very important to consider as confounding factors when testing minority students. *Data-Based Decision Making, Ethical, Legal, and Professional Foundations,* and *Applied Psychological Principles* domains.

27. **A.** The answer to this question is based on a well-known psychological theory called the halo effect. The halo effect is a confounding factor when people are engaged in formal observations. The other option choices are fictitiously created terms. *Applied Psychological Principles* domain.

28. **C.** CBM is a narrow measure and often confused with CBA. CBM's are effective tools to track student progress. CBMs supplement, not replace, standardized measures. *Data-Based Decision Making* domain.

29. **D.** The amygdala is a neurological structure that is found in the limbic system and plays a pivotal role in processing emotions. *Applied Psychological Principles* domain.

30. **C.** CBT is one of the most effective psychological interventions. Although other options are valid choices, CBT is the best answer for this question. *Research-Based Behavioral and Mental Health Practices* domain.

31. **B.** It is best practice to secure parental permission before counseling. Securing permission helps prevent conflict and builds collaboration. *Ethical, Legal, and*

*Professional Foundations* and *Research-Based Behavioral and Mental Health Practices* domains.

**32. A.** This question has several distracter options. Remember that collaboration is a key term and many choices that have this term are usually the correct answer. *Consultation and Collaboration* domain.

**33. A.** Although there are exceptions, NASP typically does not endorse grade retention. *Research-Based Academic Practices* domain.

**34. C.** Although the norms of the UNIT are old, typically nonverbal tests are appropriate for deaf students or ESL students. *Data-Based Decision Making* domain.

**35. A.** This answer is straightforward and fact based. Even if you have never heard of "in vivo" therapy, the words "flooding techniques" should give you the best clue to the correct answer. *Research-Based Behavioral and Mental Health Practices* domain.

**36. B.** To answer this question, you have to know Erikson's stages. It might be helpful to know the associated age ranges for these stages and especially the key traits of each stage. *Applied Psychological Principles* and *Research-Based Behavioral and Mental Health Practices* domains.

**37. B.** The first step in this situation is to support the family members. The second step is to provide support to classmates and friends. *Research-Based Behavioral and Mental Health Practices* domain.

**38. A.** The answer is fairly straightforward. Typically, the lower the number of students a supervisor must manage the better. *Ethical, Legal, and Professional Foundations* domain.

**39. C.** IDEA outlines Child Find services. *Ethical, Legal, and Professional Foundations* domain.

**40. B.** Alfred Binet is credited as creating one of the first standardized intelligent tests for children. *Ethical, Legal, and Professional Foundations* domain.

**41. B.** Projective tests are effective measures, but a high degree of skill and training are involved. It is good practice to supplement test results when using projective measures. *Data-Based Decision Making* domain.

**42. C.** Section 504 is an ADA law and governed by the OCR. *Ethical, Legal, and Professional Foundations* domain.

**43. C.** One of the primary reasons cognitive assessments are administered to students who are struggling academically is to predict academic performance and to help determine the appropriate level of curriculum. *Data-Based Decision Making* domain.

**44. A.** In low-level cases of ethical violation, it is acceptable to address the situation at the direct level with the person. *Ethical, Legal, and Professional Foundations* domain.

**45. C.** This is a difficult question to answer. Note that test protocols cannot be copied and parents cannot be allowed to copy information taken from a test protocol. Psychologists should fully explain their reasoning and educate parents about what scores mean without violating laws. *Data-Based*

*Decision Making, Consultation and Collaboration,* and *Ethical, Legal, and Professional Foundations* domains.

**46. B.** Parents can always use private testing, but schools do not always have to pay for such testing. Only in special circumstances are schools required to pay for outside testing. *Ethical, Legal, and Professional Foundations* domain.

**47. B.** When safety or crisis situations arise, psychologists have more flexibility to meet with students. You do not need permission in this situation. *Ethical, Legal, and Professional Foundations* and *Research-Based Behavioral and Mental Health Practices* domains.

**48. A.** It is best practice to set your rules and limitations of counseling as early as possible in the therapeutic relationship. *Research-Based Behavioral and Mental Health Practices* domain.

**49. B.** Asking clarifying questions when differences in results are discovered may illuminate the reasons for the differences. Results are not necessarily invalid just because differences exist, but you should find out why differences exist. *Data-Based Decision Making* domain.

**50. A.** A child cannot change schools or placement when a due process proceeding has commenced. *Ethical, Legal, and Professional Foundations* domain.

**51. A.** The only other possible answer to this question is C, but student eligibility for special education services is typically discussed during the initial staffing (not referral) meeting. *Ethical, Legal, and Professional Foundations* domain.

**52. A.** This simple question might be difficult to answer. Although option C might also be a good answer, the point of a school psychologist's assessment is to determine how a child functions in a *typical* school day. *Data-Based Decision Making* domain.

**53. D.** The answer is factual. You must know the correct terms to describe specific disorders. For example, do not be misled by official-sounding terms, such as fetal alcohol disorder, because there is no such disability. FAE is the correct terminology. *Research-Based Behavioral and Mental Health Practices* domain.

**54. A.** Sometimes you will have a few easy questions. The answer to this question is straightforward, but always double check your answer and re-read the question for seemingly simple items. *Applied Psychological Principles* domain.

**55. D.** The broader the score the more valid and reliable it is. *Data-Based Decision Making* domain.

**56. D.** This question is a difficult question to answer if you do not know the research related to motivation. Note that tangible rewards, while effective in some situations, may hinder the development of intrinsic motivation. Cognitive approaches are best to use to build intrinsic motivation. "Choice" is a cognitive approach that gives students control to develop preferences. *Applied Psychological Principles* and *Research-Based Academic Practices* domains.

**57. A.** Block design tasks can measure several different cognitive functions, but from a neuropsychological perspective, visual perception tasks (e.g., block design) usually activate the right regions of the brain. *Applied Psychological Principles* domain.

**58. C.** Punishment and negative reinforcement are commonly confused. Remember, any intervention that *increases* a behavior is related to negative reinforcement. *Applied Psychological Principles* and *Research-Based Academic Practices* domains.

**59. C.** Children who have dysgraphia have difficulty in writing coherently. Multiple-choice tests are a typical and appropriate accommodation for this disorder. *Research-Based Academic Practices* and *Applied Psychological Principles* domains.

**60. C.** Although the answer to this question could be debated, stimulus fading is an effective method used specifically with students that demonstrate selective mutism. Stimulus fading is related to gradual sensitization techniques. *Applied Psychological Principles* and *Research-Based Behavioral and Mental Health Practices* domains.

**61. B.** The best answer to this question is B, although D is also a possibility. Choice B is the better answer because it addresses both the positive and negative interventions involved in shaping behavior. *Applied Psychological Principles* and *Research-Based Academic Practices* domains.

**62. B.** The APA typically gives full endorsement only to PhD-level psychologists. NASP recognizes and endorses both EdS- and PhD-level school psychologists. *Ethical, Legal, and Professional Foundations* domain.

**63. C.** This is a difficult situation and a difficult question to answer. Only a judge can legally order a psychologist to turn over protocols that are copyright protected. In this situation, it is best to collaborate with the parents and explain your results to them. If parents and the lawyer persist in their demands, contact the school's lawyer. *Ethical, Legal, and Professional Foundations* and *Consultation and Collaboration* domains.

**64. D.** FERPA is related to confidentiality issues and parent access to school records. *Ethical, Legal, and Professional Foundations* domain.

**65. A.** This is not a common test question, but psychologists must be aware that copyright laws impact their practices as much as educational laws. *Ethical, Legal, and Professional Foundations* domain.

**66. A.** Planning is one of the traits associated with the concept of executive functioning. Organization and emotional and behavioral regulation are other traits of executive functioning. *Applied Psychological Principles* domain.

**67. D.** Prevention is primary in crisis intervention. Use the alliteration, prevention primary, to help you remember this concept. *Research-Based Behavioral and Mental Health Practices* domain.

**68. B.** The consultee is typically the teacher. When you employ a consultee-centered model, you are teaching the teacher to help herself. *Consultation and Collaboration* domain.

**69. C.** Although choice A may seem like a good answer, the better answer is C because it incorporates the key aspects of choice A and is more thorough. *Research-Based Behavioral and Mental Health Practices* domain.

**70. A.** Answer A is factual and most accurate. Authentic assessments do not use standardized psychometrics. *Data-Based Decision Making* domain.

**71. A.** Although there are several motivations for behavior, choice A provides the primary reasons for behavior. All other options are not necessarily supported in the literature. *Applied Psychological Principles* and *Research-Based Behavioral and Mental Health Practices* domains.

**72. C.** The two key terms in Erikson's stage described in this question are industry versus inferiority. You should memorize the five stages relevant to school-aged students. Note that the answer to this question could be found on an earlier test item on this test (#36). *Applied Psychological Principles* and *Research-Based Academic Practices* domains.

**73. B.** The approval of others and social pressure are hallmark traits of the conventional level of moral reasoning. *Applied Psychological Principles* domain.

**74. A.** On most cognitive assessments, a standard score of 90 is on the borderline between low average and below average. *Data-Based Decision Making* domain.

**75. D.** Although the student in this situation needs counseling due to her harassment, a threat of violence warrants specific legal obligations and actions from school staff. The duty to warn is a key obligation psychologists must fulfill. *Ethical, Legal, and Professional Foundations* domain.

**76. A.** Although choice C is a good choice, the best choice would be A because it is a more comprehensive intervention that would also incorporate a survey as mentioned in C. Note that D is not a good option because is supports suspensions. *Research-Based Behavioral and Mental Health Practices* domain.

**77. C.** People with an external-locus-of-control attitude do not believe they have control over events that happen to them. Students with this orientation often develop a learned-helplessness disposition. *Research-Based Academic Practices, Research-Based Behavioral and Mental Health Practices,* and *Applied Psychological Principles* domains.

**78. B.** Due to the parent's actions, the child will have difficulty developing confidence in her abilities. Only through concerted effort can genuine achievement and confidence be created. *Research-Based Academic Practices, Research-Based Behavioral and Mental Health Practices,* and *Applied Psychological Principles* domains.

**79. D.** School staff are mandated reporters and must notify police or protective services when they suspect abuse. *Ethical, Legal, and Professional Foundations* domain.

**80. A.** In the spirit of RTI, interventions should be implemented before a formal special education evaluation is started. Many times, students will respond appropriately to interventions and are not found to be disabled. *Research-Based Academic Practices* domains.

**81. A.** Although some practitioners may debate the answer to this question, it is legal and sometimes appropriate to let parents know about the research regarding medication if your assessment data supports your comments. As long as the psychologist is recommending that the parent only speak with a doctor and is not giving a direct suggestion to take medications, then this action is permissible. *Ethical, Legal, and Professional Foundations* and *Consultation and Collaboration* domains.

**82. B.** Working memory is the ability to hold information "online" while performing another task. *Applied Psychological Principles* domain.

**83. A.** Students with Asperger syndrome may also have some of the traits listed as other choices, but the hallmark trait of Asperger is social skills deficits. *Applied Psychological Principles* and *Research-Based Behavioral and Mental Health Practices* domains.

**84. B.** Mandated reporters must notify police or social services. Even if mandated reports "tell" the school social worker or principal, they are ultimately responsible to make the report to the proper authorities. *Ethical, Legal, and Professional Foundations* domain.

**85. A.** Although a child's brain can make a complete recovery after a brain injury, it is more vulnerable to permanent damage than an adult's in most cases. Brain injuries can produce learning, behavioral, emotional, and attention problems. TBI assessment is a growing responsibility for school psychologists. *Applied Psychological Principles* domain.

**86. C.** This question has several distracter answers. Phonemic awareness is the ability to manipulate sounds. For example, say cat, then say it again without the /c/ sound. *Research-Based Academic Practices* domain.

**87. A.** A FBA is the standard formal evaluation that specifically evaluates the antecedents, behavior, and consequences. *Applied Psychological Principles* and *Research-Based Academic Practices* domains.

**88. D.** The occipital lobe is considered the primary anatomical region of the visual cortex. *Applied Psychological Principles* domain.

**89. C.** There are several types of attention described in mainstream research. Attention can be divided into selective, sustained, and divided subtypes. *Applied Psychological Principles* domain.

**90. A.** Modeling is the proper psychological term to describe learning through observation. Reference Albert Bandura's work related to modeling. *Ethical, Legal, and Professional Foundations* and *Research-Based Behavioral and Mental Health Practices* domains.

**91. C.** This question is factual and straightforward. See question #90. *Ethical, Legal, and Professional Foundations* and *Research-Based Behavioral and Mental Health Practices* domains.

**92. B.** Remember that a negative correlation can be stronger than a positive correlation. Note that a -.98 is almost a perfect (i.e., highest possible) correlation. *Applied Psychological Principles* and *Data-Based Decision Making* domains.

**93. A.** Students are typically confused by this question. The experimental group is the one that is exposed to the conditions of the experiment. *Applied Psychological Principles* domain.

**94. C.** The control group is *not* exposed to experimental factors. See question #93 as a comparison. *Applied Psychological Principles* domain.

**95. C.** The correct term is *independent variable*, not *experimental variable*. Make sure you know the subtle differences between terms with these types of questions. Most students misunderstand the terms independent and dependent variables. *Applied Psychological Principles* domain.

**96. C.** NASP endorses and encourages the use of both formal and informal measures when evaluating a student for special education services. *Ethical, Legal, and Professional Foundations* and *Data-Based Decision Making* domains.

**97. A.** The term *aphasia* is associated with a range of language problems, such as word-retrieval difficulties and verbal comprehension trouble. *Applied Psychological Principles* and *Research-Based Academic Practices* domains.

**98. D.** While the other choices are reasonable answers, the best answer is a heuristic. A heuristic is a tool used in problem solving and is based on reducing the number of factors to consider. *Applied Psychological Principles* and *Research-Based Academic Practices* domains.

**99. C.** When students are asked to describe their reasoning, they are forced to interrogate their thoughts and to think deeply. Such techniques increase understanding and comprehension. *Research-Based Academic Practices* domain.

**100. A.** Note that this question, or concepts related to it, was asked in a previous question on this test. Sometimes, you can answer questions by remembering previous items. Reference question #27. *Applied Psychological Principles* domain.

**101. C.** Psychologists cannot be asked to violate their ethical code of conduct. Handling this case at the lowest level first, before higher level actions are pursued, is best practice. *Ethical, Legal, and Professional Foundations* domain.

**102. A.** CBM is not a norm-referenced measurement tool. It is effective in the RTI process and allows staff to monitor progress toward educational goals. *Research-Based Academic Practices* domain.

**103. B.** When meeting with students, you only need permission from the parents and should secure such permission before counseling starts. Although it might be important to notify relevant staff and administration, it is not required. *Ethical, Legal, and Professional Foundations* and *Consultation and Collaboration* domains.

**104. B.** Child Find is a provision and terminology used in IDEA law that mandates schools to actively seek out children with disabilities. *Ethical, Legal, and Professional Foundations* domain.

**105. D.** Although the CAS by Naglieri and Das is somewhat dated, students might benefit from knowing who A.E. Luria is and his landmark work. Luria's work forms the basis for many neuropsychological theories. *Data-Based Decision Making, Applied Psychological Principles,* and *Ethical, Legal, and Professional Foundations* domains.

106. **C.** Humanists, such as Rogers and Maslow, are central figures who believed people have an innate desire for growth. *Research-Based Behavioral and Mental Health Practices* and *Ethical, Legal, and Professional Foundations* domains.

107. **D.** The CHC theory is a well-established and accepted statistical theory that supports many mainstream cognitive tests. Fluid and crystallized abilities are primary domains of the CHC theory. *Data-Based Decision Making* and *Applied Psychological Principles* domains.

108. **A.** Although the lower the number, the better, NASP generally supports that psychologists should serve no more than 1,000 students. *Ethical, Legal, and Professional Foundations* domain.

109. **D.** It is important that you can differentiate between autism and Asperger syndrome. Many features of Asperger syndrome are not as severe as autism. *Research-Based Behavioral and Mental Health Practices* and *Applied Psychological Principles* domains.

110. **B.** Typically, self-awareness and perspective training are difficult for students with Asperger syndrome or autism. Although the previous techniques are still effective, the best answer for this question is B. *Research-Based Behavioral and Mental Health Practices* and *Applied Psychological Principles* domains.

111. **C.** Children with Asperger syndrome often qualify for special education services because their social skills deficits impede their ability to make and maintain social relationships. *Research-Based Behavioral and Mental Health Practices* and *Applied Psychological Principles* domains.

112. **A.** It is best practice to evaluate the frequency, intensity, and duration of a behavior when asked to conduct formal observations. *Research-Based Behavioral and Mental Health Practices* domain.

113. **B.** According to the CDC, the prevalence rate for learning disabilities is approximately 7.6 %. Note the range this statistic falls between in the given choices. *Research-Based Academic Practices* and *Ethical, Legal, and Professional Foundations* domains.

114. **C.** The standard convention related to the gifted range of standard scores is approximately 130 (125 to 135). *Data-Based Decision Making* domain.

115. **A.** A student should be afforded the same opportunities as provided to the general student population. *Ethical, Legal, and Professional Foundations* domain.

116. **A.** Research in this area suggests there is no definitive profile of a school shooter, although there are traits and incidences to consider as risk factors. Reference the *Safe School Initiative* provided by the government. *Research-Based Behavioral and Mental Health Practices* domain.

117. **B.** In most cases, the best approach to teaching students is by using an array of different approaches that hold their interest and may cover their learning preferences. *Research-Based Academic Practices* domain.

118. **B.** This answer is factual and straightforward. Narrative recording contains a running record and notes on a student. *Research-Based Academic Practices* domain.

119. **B.** NASP has a positive view of homeschooled children but also supports a healthy collaboration among all parties involved in a child's learning. *Ethical, Legal, and Professional Foundations* and *Consultation and Collaboration* domains.

120. **D.** Simultaneous processing is a neurocognitive process and term used by school-neuropsychologists. *Data-Based Decision Making* and *Applied Psychological Principles* domains.


# Practice Test II

1. **C.** Although all choices are valid, NASP does not generally endorse grade retention. *Data-Based Decision Making* domain.

2. **A.** Semi-structured interviews have validity because the interview questions are standardized and asked of all interviewees. This method also allows for the interviewer to ask follow-up questions, unlike the structured interview method. Note that option C sounds legitimate, but this response is not a valid term. *Data-Based Decision Making* domain.

3. **B.** In the scenario, the referral question is vague and the student's specific area of struggle is unknown. It is good practice to define the problem as specifically as possible before targeting interventions or assessments. Note that A and D are good choices but are not the first step. The student may not be in the RTI process and the referral may be a step in placing the student in the RTI system once areas of difficulty are defined. *Data-Based Decision Making* domain.

4. **A.** Interval sampling is a good choice because it is a time efficient method, especially when it is difficult to determine when a behavior begins or ends. *Data-Based Decision Making* domain.

5. **C.** Generally, there are three levels of analysis: variability, level, and trend. *Data-Based Decision Making* domain.

6. **B.** A trend is a collection of data points that show a decrease or increase in performance across time. *Data-Based Decision Making* domain.

7. **D.** Although it could be argued that any other response is a good answer, the best answer is D because confounding variables should always be considered when analyzing any type of collected data. A confounding factor could be related to the student's learning and development. *Data-Based Decision Making* domain.

8. **B.** This is a difficult question to answer because the first three responses could arguably be correct. However the *best* answer for the given scenario is B. A change of instruction would be acceptable, but the last data point does show positive movement. An appropriate response would be a modification in the intervention but not to change it significantly at this point. *Data-Based Decision Making* domain.

9. **C.** Although SES (socioeconomic status) can be a confounding factor in some academic cases, it is typically not a solitary factor and it is considered with several other confounding variables. Notice how the other three correct answers focus narrowly on the analysis of the data set. *Data-Based Decision Making* domain.

10. **B.** Best practice and legal mandates clearly state that practitioners must use a variety of sources that include formal and informal measures. Although valid and reliable data (choice A) is a good choice, such terms are generally used to describe only standardized and formal measures. Also, choice C has the word "tests" and informal measures are typically not tests. *Data-Based Decision Making* domain.

11. **C.** School psychologists must provide a cognitive assessment and adaptive-functional assessments. Note that you do not have to know the names of these tests if other terms in the choices describe the nature of the test. *Data-Based Decision Making* domain.

12. **A.** Baseline data should not have significant variability in performance. Baseline data collection is not time driven, as seen in response option B, but one should collect at least three data points. Note that the last two options are not valid. *Data-Based Decision Making* domain.

13. **D.** Although all the other processes listed might be included on major neuropsychological assessments, processing speed is considered a basal neurological function and is considered an ability rather than a skill that is influenced by exposure to particular information. Remember, if you see the term "reasoning," this implies a higher order process. *Data-Based Decision Making* domain.

14. **D.** Although response C is also a good option, the BASC combined with an FBA will provide formal and informal data. *Data-Based Decision Making* domain.

15. **B.** Although only a few steps are listed for each choice, the FBA process starts with defining the problem, then other steps follow. Also, the hypothesis for the behavior is based on the observation and only option B has this step in the correct order. *Data-Based Decision Making* domain.

16. **C.** Current guidelines encourage an emphasis on the antecedent and environmental modifications over consequences to modify student behavior. This is not to state that consequences are not important to consider, but many times it is easy and effective to modify a student's immediate environment first before more complex strategies are used. *Data-Based Decision Making* domain.

17. **B.** CBA is broader than a CBM, which may include specific measurements such as CBM. Because CBM's are narrow in scope, C and D could not be the *best* answer. *Data-Based Decision Making* domain.

18. **C.** CBM is a measurement tool that typically references a class (i.e., local) norm and the test material is taken directly from the child's curriculum. *Data-Based Decision Making* domain.

**19. D.** The standard criteria for an intellectual disability (formally SLIC), is deficient adaptive functional scores and a standard score of 70 or below on cognitive test measures. *Data-Based Decision Making* domain.

**20. C.** Although choice B is correct, the best response is C because it includes critical informal data as well information taken from formal tests that are normed appropriately. *Data-Based Decision Making* domain.

**21. A.** The halo effect is a well-known observer bias that is a confounding factor when observing people. This factor was heavily researched by Edward Thorndike. *Data-Based Decision Making* domain.

**22. C.** Although choices "A" and "B" are sometimes true, there are some brief projective measures that do not involve lengthy training or time to administer. Also remember that all tests are subject to confounding factors. Reliability statistics are generally lower on projective measures compared to standardized tests. *Data-Based Decision Making* domain.

**23. B.** All other responses have one term that is not a valid response choice. *Data-Based Decision Making* domain.

**24. B.** Test interpretation should begin from broad scores because these scores are the most valid and reliable. Item and subtest interpretation generally does not have the validity of broader scores. C and D are not good choices because it is important to report the pattern of strengths and weaknesses. *Data-Based Decision Making* domain.

**25. D.** All of the other choices are effective features of PBS. While choice D has validity, it is not the best response. *Research-Based Behavioral and Mental Health Practices* domain.

**26. B.** While a large number of students are harassed, recent research indicates it is not over 50%. *Research-Based Behavioral and Mental Health Practices* domain.

**27. C.** Zero tolerance policies are discouraged. Schools should try to re-educate students who harass and bully other students. A psychologist's role is to remediate and educate, not punish. *Research-Based Behavioral and Mental Health Practices* domain.

**28. C.** While counseling is effective and may be part of a corrective measure, the bully should make amends with the victims in a positive manner. *Research-Based Behavioral and Mental Health Practices* domain.

**29. D.** If you talk with another mental health professional, the student's identity must be kept secret or you should not talk about cases. Option D does not provide information about confidentiality during the consultation. Danger and safety to self or others are primary causes to breach confidentiality (A and C). Also, a student can give you permission to talk with others (B). *Research-Based Behavioral and Mental Health Practices* domain.

**30. A.** Choice B is not a real therapy. C is not practiced in schools and D is a general approach rather than a specific technique. CBT is widely regarded as an effective counseling method. *Research-Based Behavioral and Mental Health Practices* domain.

31. **C.** Although all of the response choices are valid, answer C best describes Skinner's belief. Note that answer C is broader than the other choices and the word "consequences" covers both positive and negative reinforcements that may shape behavior. *Research-Based Behavioral and Mental Health Practices* domain.

32. **D.** Service learning includes teaching students in the authentic environment and is typically used to build empathy in students. *Research-Based Behavioral and Mental Health Practices* domain.

33. **A.** Applied behavior analysis (ABA) and intervention is an effective approach with students who have autism. ABA includes the key aspects of task analysis and a highly structured and systematic means of teaching new skills. The other choices may contain valid terms, but the other choice options are not completely valid names. Note that the question has extraneous information that acts as a distracter (e.g., ADHD). *Research-Based Behavioral and Mental Health Practices* domain.

34. **C.** The first three choices are all valid, but C is the best choice because it includes fading techniques. Once a behavior is taught using a highly structured and systematic means, the prompts must be slowly removed so the student can be independent. *Research-Based Behavioral and Mental Health Practices* domain.

35. **B.** All responses to this question are valid; however, the best way to approach crisis is to work to prevent a crisis situation from happening in the first place. Practice and preparation are key aspects of crisis plans. *Research-Based Behavioral and Mental Health Practices* domain.

36. **B.** PTSD is a primary concern after exposure to a traumatic event. PTSD symptoms are varied, but center on hyper-arousal, over-alertness, anxiety, avoidance, and obsessive thoughts about the incident. *Research-Based Behavioral and Mental Health Practices* domain.

37. **C.** While it is important to notify parents and your school administrator of the assessment, it is *most* critical that you never leave a potentially suicidal student alone. *Research-Based Behavioral and Mental Health Practices* domain.

38. **D.** Although it is important to talk with staff as soon as possible and provide support to the family and peers of the student, it is primary to first plan for contagion effects and prevent dangerous copycat actions by others. *Research-Based Behavioral and Mental Health Practices* domain.

39. **D.** Choice A may seem like a good answer—only facts should be provided to others. However, too many details about a suicide are not necessarily a good idea, especially for younger students. Although rumor control is an important consideration, an announcement to all students and staff over a public announcement system is not an endorsed practiced. C is not a valid choice. *Research-Based Behavioral and Mental Health Practices* domain.

40. **A.** The preoperational stage covers the age range between 2 to 7 years old. The hallmark feature of this stage is the emergence of simple symbolic thinking. For example, a picture of a cat is known by the student to

represent a real cat. Option D is fictitious. *Applied Psychological Principles* domain.

**41. C.** The typical age range for students within the identity versus role confusion stage is 13 to 18 years old. Although the age range for stage theories is important to consider, it is most important to consider the aspects that define particular stages. In the question, the gifted and talented description is not a significant consideration. It can be inferred that the student's occupational path provides a sense of identity. *Applied Psychological Principles* domain.

**42. C.** All of the choices are valid psychological experts. Albert Bandura believed in the cognitive component of learning and he believed that people can learn by watching others. His beliefs were in contrast to the principles of behaviorism. Bandura is also known for his famous bobo doll study involving violence. *Applied Psychological Principles* domain.

**43. D.** Given an approximate standard error of measurement of plus or minus 5 points, a full scale standard score of 113 would situate the true score within the average to above average range (108 to 118). Most major tests have a standard score range of 85 to 115 as average. Standard scores typically near 110 are considered high average. *Applied Psychological Principles* domain.

**44. B.** A T-score of 65 or more is near the clinically significant range (e.g., 1.5 standards above the mean). Although the two scores are cause for concern, more information from observations and other measures is necessary to make professional judgments. The BASC is a good tool, but it is only one source of data and the NASP endorses multiple sources of information in formal situations. *Applied Psychological Principles* domain.

**45. A.** Although all choices could be valid, the choice that would complete a comprehensive evaluation is A. A review of student records involves both previous academic and behavioral information. Also, A is the only choice that has a student observation, which is key for initial evaluations. *Applied Psychological Principles* domain.

**46. C.** Kohlberg used the term "preconventional" to describe the stage of moral development that is based on the desire to avoid punishment and gain rewards. It is important to remember that stage theories might have age ranges attached to them, but it might be better to understand the defining characteristics of a particular stage than it is to memorize age ranges. Note that choices A and D are fictitious and invalid terms. *Applied Psychological Principles* domain.

**47. D.** The prevalence of ADHD is approximately 3% to 7% of the population. Although ADHD might be over-diagnosed, this statement is more professional opinion than a research-based response. Answer C might be a valid response, but D is the best answer supported by research. *Applied Psychological Principles* domain.

**48. C.** Anxiety is a central feature of PTSD. Most individuals with PTSD relive traumatic events that trigger a fight or flight response that is based on fear. Fear and lack of control over events cause anxiety. Although the other choices might also have anxiety components, it may not be the prevalent feature in all cases. For example, some people diagnosed with a personality disorder might experience very little anxiety. *Applied Psychological Principles* domain.

**49. D.** While prevalence rates will vary every few years, autism spectrum disorders (ASD) are said to be about 1 in every 88 people (Centers for Disease Control and Prevention, 2012). Keep in mind that ASD includes PDD-NOS and Asperger syndrome. If the question had asked about the prevalence rate just for autism, then the figure might be much lower. *Applied Psychological Principles* domain.

**50. B.** It is inferred that Deb is already being screened for dyslexia due to the formal referral related to reading. The new information indicates that she may also have a quantitative reasoning problem that is the hallmark feature of dyscalculia. *Applied Psychological Principles* domain.

**51. A.** The Theory of the Mind is the appropriate name of a specific theory associated with the perspective-taking difficulties associated with autism. *Applied Psychological Principles* domain.

**52. B.** Learned helplessness is a term used by Dr. Martin Seligman. People who believe that they have little control over events in life typically develop a learned helplessness perspective. People with learned helplessness attitudes do not have positive outcomes. *Applied Psychological Principles* domain.

**53. C.** The Premack Principle is a well-known behavioral tenet related to B. F. Skinner's theories. The Premack Principle states that a higher desired behavior can shape a lower desired behavior. *Applied Psychological Principles* domain.

**54. B.** Negative reinforcement can increase a target behavior and is typically confused with the term *punishment* because punishments also uses negative means to achieve its goal. On the other hand, punishment uses negative means in an attempt to decrease a behavior (e.g., spanking a child to decrease stealing). To help with the distinction between terms, think of the annoying seatbelt reminder noise in a car. The noise is a negative stimulus designed to *increase* your seatbelt-buckling behavior. *Applied Psychological Principles* domain.

**55. C.** Variable reinforcement schedules are effective because the participants do not know when they will be rewarded. Once established, the participants are likely to continue the behavior because they do not know when the specific behavior will be reinforced, so they will continue the behavior in the hope that each behavior will result in a reward. Variable reinforcement behaviors are difficult to extinguish once established. *Applied Psychological Principles* domain.

**56. D.** Major cognitive tests, such as the latest versions of the WISC and DAS, are constructed upon a sophisticated statistical theory known as the Cattell–Horn–Carroll (CHC) theory. The first two choices are named after famous psychometricians, but their names are not used as terms for specific theories. *Applied Psychological Principles* domain.

**57. B.** Syntax is related to the rules governing how words and sentences are constructed, including the order of words. Semantics involves word meanings and is not a correct response. The correct syntax in the given example, should be, "We go to the car." Phonological and phonemic concepts involve the sound structure of words and language, not the order of words. *Applied Psychological Principles* domain.

**58. C.** This question is one of the few test items that straightforwardly asks for the name of a specific person. All choices are well-known psychological theorists, but Noam Chomsky is known for his work on language acquisition. *Applied Psychological Principles* domain.

**59. A.** Criterion-referenced tests are also known as domain-referenced tests and are defined by mastery of standard or defined skills. Norm-referenced tests are the opposite of criterion-based tests. Choice C is a fictitious and invalid response. *Applied Psychological Principles* domain.

**60. D.** The mean, or average, is found by adding all the numbers in a set of numbers, then dividing by the total numbers given in the set. In the case provided, the sum of the set is 30. There are 5 numbers given. Dividing 30 by 5 equals 6. *Applied Psychological Principles* domain.

**61. A.** The mode is the most frequently occurring number in a set of numbers. Choices B and C are not valid, whereas D is considered the range. Although not given, the median is the middle number of a data set. *Applied Psychological Principles* domain.

**62. D.** The first two choices are not valid responses to this question because reliability involves the consistence of test items and performance across time. One method of determining validity is found by comparing a test to another test that measures the same underlying trait. It is important to understand the difference between validity and reliability. *Applied Psychological Principles* domain.

**63. C.** All of the other choices are valid responses. Choice C might be a common practice, but the research regarding homework is variable and is not best response given the other choices for this item. *Research-Based Academic Practices* domain.

**64. A.** The terms *practice* and *application* found in the other choices are not valid. *Research-Based Academic Practices* domain.

**65. B.** This question is difficult to answer because it is specific. Key terms to remember are **explicit** and **systematic**. *Research-Based Academic Practices* domain.

**66. C.** When teachers differentiate instruction, they directly address the individual differences, abilities, and needs of individual learners. All other choices except B are valid teaching methods but not relevant to the question. *Research-Based Academic Practices* domain.

**67. A.** While other choices are valid and might be good responses, the *best* response would be A. Family involvement and educational support provided by parents can offset the factors associated with SES or poverty. *Research-Based Academic Practices* domain.

**68. C.** Grade retention in general is not an endorsed practice. Although D is a good choice, it should be only given after additional information is gathered on the problem. *Research-Based Academic Practices* domain.

**69. D.** D is a fictitious and invalid response item. All other choices are correct responses. Remember, the role of school is to educate students, not punish them harshly. *Research-Based Academic Practices* domain.

**70. B.** B is a good choice because it includes both an increase in personal skills and knowledge of others. A is also a good choice, but it does not include an increase in academic skills. C is not necessarily accurate because some cooperative lessons are more time intensive than other methods. D is a very good option, but research related to cooperative learning does not necessarily focus on increasing sympathy. *Research-Based Academic Practices* domain.

**71. C.** Token economies are effective in changing behaviors, but busy teachers have difficulty collecting data and rewarding students immediately after a desired behavior. Token economies are effective with all ages and are typically not too expensive to employ. If fading is done properly with a cognitive component, then the target behavior can be maintained after tokens are withdrawn. *Research-Based Academic Practices* domain.

**72. A.** The key words in the question are large projects. If students do not have problems in other classes and behavior is not a concern, then it should be suspect that the students have difficulty with long, complicated information. A task analysis is a critical component that is necessary to know where to break assignments into easier steps. Referral to the RTI process is generally a more involved process and a full remediation program may not be appropriate in this situation if a simple fix will suffice. *Research-Based Academic Practices* domain.

**73. B.** SQ3R stands for survey, question, read, recite, and review. This method asks the reader to activate his knowledge of the text and to create questions before reading, which increases metacognition. Linda-Mood-Bell and Wilson programs are well-known reading interventions but aren't necessarily focused on reading comprehension like SQ3R. Also, psychologists initially recommend specific strategies for particular learning difficulties rather than comprehensive remediation programs. *Research-Based Academic Practices* domain.

**74. C.** It is important to know the difference between an accommodation and remediation. Remediation changes the task or curriculum, whereas accommodation changes the environment and/or conditions under which the task is completed. However, there is some debate about the exact nature of these concepts. Allowing for extra time does not change the academic task to be completed, but accommodates for the time that it must be finished. If you allow a student to read a lower level passage, this intervention changes the task that is required to be completed by other students. Answer A might be construed as a spelling intervention, not a reading accommodation. *Research-Based Academic Practices* domain.

**75. D.** This answer is straightforward. All other choices are fictitious and invalid. *Research-Based Academic Practices* domain.

76. **A.** Although all the other choices are valid, the best choice would be A. The key words in the question are "personality traits." Choices B and C are more aligned with skills rather than personality traits. *Consultation and Collaboration* domain.

77. **C.** This is one of those seemingly simple questions that takes time to answer. Although all choices may seem valid, a staff member's intelligence is not typically a consideration in collaboration. It is assumed that most staff members (e.g., teachers) have average intelligence and are college educated. *Consultation and Collaboration* domain.

78. **A.** The *consultee* is a term that generally describes the teacher. The Consultee model is a favored model of consultation because it teaches the teacher to solve future problems. The client is a student. *Consultation and Collaboration* domain.

79. **D.** When the consultant provides direct services to the client (e.g., student), this is an example of the client model. *Consultation and Collaboration* domain.

80. **A.** In the conjoint behavioral model, the focus is on the behavior of the student and the consultation involves a joint effort among all parties. Choice D may sound valid, but it is a fictitious term. *Consultation and Collaboration* domain.

81. **B.** The behavioral consultation model starts with clearly defining the problem. Once a problem behavior is defined, the next steps can be implemented, such as data collection and creating a plan. *Consultation and Collaboration* domain.

82. **D.** There are many barriers to effective consultation and other professional relationships that school psychologists face. The first three are valid choices. Consultation sometimes involves a heavy time commitment due to communication and scheduling issues. However, financial considerations are not a normal concern in most cases. *Consultation and Collaboration* domain.

83. **C.** Teaching other staff members how to solve problems for themselves is an effective and time efficient practice in the long term. Consultee-centered models are endorsed by NASP. *Consultation and Collaboration* domain.

84. **D.** The first two choices can be easily ruled as invalid. C is a little more difficult, but a police officer cannot make a psychologist disclose information, such as grades, that may not be pertinent to a situation. Answer D involves safety and harm, which always trump confidentiality laws. *Ethical, Legal, and Professional Foundations* domain.

85. **B.** If the psychologist in this situation is qualified and licensed to engage in private practice, then she can accept this type of work. One of the reasons this type of work is ethical to accept is because school districts are not required to test students so they can apply for private school. If the student had a suspected disability, then the psychologist could not accept this work because that is covered by public schools. Testing students when a

disability is suspected is covered by a public school psychologist and should not be conducted for a charge. *Ethical, Legal, and Professional Foundations* domain.

**86. C.** The answer to this question is straightforward. *Ethical, Legal, and Professional Foundations* domain.

**87. C.** In cases that do not involve danger or safety, practitioners should try to solve the problem at the lowest level possible, but they are obligated to file a formal complaint if the problem is not solved. *Ethical, Legal, and Professional Foundations* domain.

**88. D.** Only state authorities can revoke the license of a legally licensed practitioner. Although NASP has authority that governs membership privileges, it does not have legal enforcement powers. *Ethical, Legal, and Professional Foundations* domain.

**89. B.** Although aversive techniques should be avoided, there are some circumstances that involve safety in which such techniques are appropriate. For example, a student is actively cutting himself in your office and you must physically restrain the child for his safety. *Ethical, Legal, and Professional Foundations* domain.

**90. C.** Although choice A is also a very good response, to make sure you are following state laws regarding child abuse reporting, it is good practice to seek consultation while maintaining anonymity for the student. *Ethical, Legal, and Professional Foundations* domain.

**91. C.** Special education students can be suspended, but if the suspension totals more than 10 days, a review meeting must be held to determine whether the behavior plan is appropriate and other needs or obligations of the student are being addressed. *Ethical, Legal, and Professional Foundations* domain.

**92. B.** LRE or least restrictive environment states, "To the maximum extent appropriate, children with disabilities should be educated with children who are not disabled, and special classes, separate schooling, or other removal of children with disabilities from the regular educational environment should occur only when the nature or severity of the disability is such that education in regular classes with the use of supplementary aids and services cannot be achieved satisfactorily." Note all other choices are fictitious. *Ethical, Legal, and Professional Foundations* domain.

**93. C.** Choice C is correct. FERPA was created to safeguard educational records. Note that FERPA was established in 1974 and option B was an invalid distracter. *Ethical, Legal, and Professional Foundations* domain.

**94. D.** Section 504 was created by the Americans with Disabilities Act (ADA) and contains a broad definition for the terms *handicap* or *disability*. Special education laws, such as IDEIA, has narrow definitions of disability and more specific criteria that must be met to be identified with a particular disability compared to Section 504. *Ethical, Legal, and Professional Foundations* domain.

**95. D.** As with many legal questions, the answer to this question can be debated. If a psychologist makes documented "good-faith" efforts to contact a parent for a triennial review, then the psychologist may proceed cautiously if parent contact fails. Additionally, the parent's complaint takes place 3 years after the event, but the law only provides a 2-year window to file a complaint. Choice A contains unknown information as well as choice B. Although C has some validity, it is the documentation of attempts that makes answer D the best answer. *Ethical, Legal, and Professional Foundations* domain.

**96. B.** The answer to this question is factual and straightforward. Once a parent signs permission to evaluate, the special education team has 60 days to complete the evaluation. *Ethical, Legal, and Professional Foundations* domain.

**97. A.** Students frequently mistake Lightner Witmer with Arnold Gessell. Although Witmer was not an option, it is important to know that Gessell is widely regarded as the first school psychologist, whereas Witmer is known as the father of school psychology. All of the other choices are not regarded as *school* psychologists, but rather they are regarded as famous experts in related fields. *Ethical, Legal, and Professional Foundations* domain.

**98. D.** Jensen is a prominent contributor to the field of psychology as it relates to intelligence. Jensen received some controversial criticism for his work, but current mainstream theory holds to his view that there is a genetic component to intelligence. *Ethical, Legal, and Professional Foundations* domain.

**99. C.** In the case of *Hobson v. Hansen*, the court ruled that schools must provide equal educational opportunities despite a family's socioeconomic status (SES). *Ethical, Legal, and Professional Foundations* domain.

**100. B.** Anytime safety or danger is an issue, confidentiality laws are trumped. Parents do not need to give consent or be present if other students are in danger. However, if a list was found with student names and a weapon was found, the parents of the students who were listed must be notified. Precedent for this situation is based on the Tarasoff case. *Ethical, Legal, and Professional Foundations* domain.

**101. B.** In the field of educational law, the famous *Brown v. Board of Education* is one of the most important cases and was responsible for mitigating discriminatory practices. All other choices are also important educational legal cases, but do not directly influence segregation. *Ethical, Legal, and Professional Foundations* domain.

**102. D.** Language in general is largely influenced by the left hemisphere and the temporal lobe. A specific area in the temporal lobe, called Broca's area, plays a critical function with expressive language. *Neuropsychology and Assessment* domain.

**103. A.** Neuropsychology is concerned with brain–behavior relationships. Although a neuropsychologist can use tests that measure higher level reasoning skills, generally speaking, neuropsychological instruments evaluate basal neuropsychological processes such as memory, attention, and processing speed. Full-scale scores from school psychology tests, such as the WISC or DAS, are very good at predicting student achievement, while neuropsychologists can pinpoint subtle areas of neurological difficulties. *Neuropsychology and Assessment* domain.

**104. B.** The brain contains several neurochemicals that are usually maintained in a tight balance. Dopamine is a well-known and critical neurochemical that must be in balance for the brain to function. Several solid studies suggest that ADHD and Parkinson's are related to low levels of dopamine. *Neuropsychology and Assessment* domain.

**105. B.** The frontal cortex of the brain plays a pivotal role in the regulation and management of behaviors associated with executive functions. *Applied Psychological Principles* domain.

**106. D.** The right hemisphere of the brain is associated with new learning and processing novel information. The left hemisphere, in general, helps with memory for learned facts, logic, and details. *Applied Psychological Principles* domain.

**107. C.** There are more elaborate depictions of the information processing model, but in its simplest forms, C best represents this cognitive process. Another way to describe this model is encode → processing → decode. Although the information processing model is still used by practitioners, researchers generally agree that the model is too simplistic. Brain processes illustrated by computer models are not entirely accurate. *Applied Psychological Principles* domain.

**108. A.** The answer is factual and straightforward. Make sure you do not confuse T-scores with standard scores. If this question asked about a standard score of 65, then the answer would be significantly different (e.g., significantly below average). *Applied Psychological Principles* domain.

**109. C.** Because the student has a *history* of reading problems, an intervention should be recommended. Special education might be an option at a later time, but because Colette has moved twice at a young age, it is likely that there is an environmental factor influencing her learning. Choice D is valid, but C is better. *Applied Psychological Principles* and *Ethical, Legal, and Professional Foundations* domains.

**110. B.** Family health and employment stability are aspects of the Safety Needs level. *Research-Based Behavioral and Mental Health Practices* domain.

**111. D.** Although modeling and role playing could be useful in all of the choices, it is most likely to be employed with students who need to develop appropriate social skills. *Research-Based Behavioral and Mental Health Practices* domain.

**112. A.** Of all the choices provided, Viktor Frankl emphasized that people have a choice in how they respond to events, even in the most difficult situations. *Research-Based Behavioral and Mental Health Practices* domain.

**113. B.** Time-out techniques are frequently used as punishment when they should be employed as preventative measures. In choice B, a student with ADHD can possibly take a cognitive break to help with his concentration and prevent negative behaviors that may develop if the student becomes too frustrated. *Research-Based Behavioral and Mental Health Practices* and *Applied Psychological Principles* domains.

**114. D.** There are three levels typically illustrated within the RTI pyramid. At the bottom level, screening and universal measures reside. Level two RTI interventions are associated with more targeted interventions for at-risk students. At the highest RTI level, the most intensive interventions are found, usually for 5% to 8% of a school's population. *Research-Based Behavioral and Mental Health Practices* domain.

**115. C.** This item might be difficult to answer because other choices are valid or have components that are valid. Remember the acronym ICEL when answering ecological types of questions. ICEL stands for instruction, curriculum, environment, and learner style. *Research-Based Behavioral and Mental Health Practices* domain.

**116. A.** Special education qualifications have strict criteria that a special education team must consider. A primary consideration by the special education team is to determine whether a student cannot access the general curriculum and if there is negative educational and/or social impact from the suspected disability. In this case, it is implied that the student is making "reasonable educational progress." There may be other ways to address the concerns of the parent. Medical doctors not employed by a school district have no authority to dictate educational services. *Research-Based Behavioral and Mental Health Practices* domains.

**117. B.** A new role for psychologists is brain injury specialist because psychologists are trained in measuring brain-based functions. Although options C and A might also be valid choices, psychologists have been involved in providing professional consultation regarding reading problems and threatening behaviors longer than brain injury management issues. *Applied Psychological Principles* and *Ethical, Legal, and Professional Foundations* domains.

**118. C.** Although this question and answer is not common to the field of school psychology, be prepared to answer such questions. Systematic desensitization is a well-known behavioral technique that is typically associated with helping people with various irrational fears. *Research-Based Behavioral and Mental Health Practices* domains.

**119. D.** Lack of sleep has been scientifically correlated with poor memory performance. Video game playing by teens is a growing concern as it is addictive to school-aged students, especially males. *Applied Psychological Principles* domain.

**120. C.** The answer to this test item is difficult because all but B are valid responses. The best answer is C because this choice includes practice and supervision. A colleague can provide insight and feedback when learning new psychological tests and practices. It is not always feasible to take a full training course on a new test, and watching a video of a new assessment does not provide enough training. *Ethical, Legal, and Professional Foundations* domain.

# Bibliography and Resources

## Bibliography

Academic Success for All Learners. (2012). *Utah students at risk: Online staff development academy*. Retrieved from www.usu.edu/teachall/text/behavior/ LRBIpdfs/Functional.pdf

Brain Injury Association of New York. (2012). *About the brain*. Retrieved from http://www.projectlearnet.org/about_the_brain.html

Brain Injury Networking Teams. (2012). TBI matrix guide. Traumatic Brain Injury Networking Team Resource Network. Retrieved from http://cokidswithbrain-injury.com/educators-and-professionals/information-matrix

Brock, S. E., Lazarus, P. J., & Jimerson, S. R. (2002). *Best practices in school crisis prevention and Intervention*. Bethesda, MD: National Association of School Psychologists.

Carter, R., Aldridge, S., Page, M., et al. (2009). *The human brain book*. New York, NY: DK Publishing.

Center on the Social and Emotional Foundations for Early Learning. (2012). Retrieved from http://csefel.vanderbilt.edu

Centers for Disease Control and Prevention (CDC). (2012). Retrieved from http://www.cdc.gov

Collaborative for Academic, Social, and Emotional Learning. (2012). Retrieved from http://www.casel.org

ETS. (2012). *Overview of the National Association of School Psychologists (NASP) Nationally Certified School Psychologist (NCSP) requirements*. Retrieved from www.ets.org/praxis/nasp

Fagan, T. K., & Wise, P. S. (2007). *School psychology: Past, present, and future* (3rd ed.). Bethesda, MD: National Association of School Psychologists.

Finkelstein, J. (n.d.). *Maslow's hierarchy of needs*. Retrieved from http://commons .wikimedia.org/wiki/File:Maslow's_hierarchy_of_needs.png

Hale, J., & Fiorello, C. A. (2004). *School neuropsychology: A practitioner's handbook*. New York, NY: Guilford Press.

Miller, D. (2007). *Essentials of school neuropsychological assessment*. Hoboken, NJ: Wiley and Sons.

National Association of School Neuropsychologists. (2012). *School neuropsychology training and resources*. Retrieved from http://www.schoolneuropsych.com

National Association of School Psychologists. (2002). *Times of tragedy: Preventing suicide in troubled children and youth, Part II*. Retrieved from http://www .nasponline.org/resources/crisis_safety/suicidept2_general.aspx

National Association of School Psychologists. (2012a). *Ethical conduct and professional practices*. Retrieved from http://www.nasponline.org/standards/ethics/ ethical-conduct-professional-practices.aspx

National Association of School Psychologists. (2012b). *NASP resources*. Retrieved from http://www.nasponline.org/resources/index.aspx

National Child Traumatic Stress Network. (2012). Retrieved from http://www .nctsn.org/about-us/national-center

National Institute of Health and Child Development (NICHD). (2012). *Helping children cope with crisis: Where can I get more information?*. Retrieved from http://www.nichd.nih.gov/publications/pubs/cope_with_crisis_book/sub12.cfm

Oritz, S. O. (2008). *Best practices in school psychology*. Bethesda, MD: National Association of School Psychologists.

Sweeney, M. (2009). *Brain: The complete mind*. Washington, DC: National Geographic Society.

Trochim, W. (2006). *The research methods knowledge base* (2nd ed.). Web center for social research methods. Retrieved from http://www.socialresearchmethods .net/kb/index.php

United States Secret Service and United States Department of Education. (2002). *Threat assessment in schools: A guide to managing threatening situations and creating safe school climates*. Retrieved from http://www.secretservice.gov/ ntac/ssi_guide.pdf

## Resources

Center for Effective Collaboration and Practice: http://cecp.air.org/default.asp

Resources for Sir Francis Galton:

Galton.org

http://www.muskingum.edu/~psych/psycweb/history/galton.htm

http://www.indiana.edu/~intell/galton.shtml

Resources for Alexandria Luria:

http://luria.ucsd.edu/

http://lchc.ucsd.edu/MCA/Mail/xmcamail.2010_02.dir/pdfhSRSAFKVs7.pdf

Resources for Jack Naglieri:

http://www.ncbi.nlm.nih.gov/pubmed/22110322

http://faculty.unlv.edu/pjones/cas_overview.pdf

http://neuhaus.org/news/dr-jack-naglieri-helping-all-children-learn/

Resources to use to review neuropsychology, basic neuroanatomy, and school neuropsychology:

School Neuropsychology Training and Resources: www.schoolneuropsych.com

Traumatic Brain Injury Networking Team Resource Network: http://cokids with-braininjury.com

# Index